The Glory of the Gospel

The Glory of the Gospel

Keswick 2005

Edited by Ali Hull

Authentic

11   10   09   08   07   06   05   7   6   5   4   3   2   1

First published 2005 by Authentic Media
9 Holdom Avenue, Bletchley, Milton Keynes, MK1 1QR
and 129 Mobilization Drive, Waynesboro, GA 30830-4575, USA
www.authenticmedia.co.uk

British Library Cataloguing in Publication Data

A catalogue record for this book is available from
the British Library

ISBN 1-85078

Cover design by fourninezero design.
Photography © Adam Greene, Nigel Cooke and Keswick Convention Council
Print Management by Adare Carwin
Printed in Great Britain by J.H. Haynes & Co., Sparkford

Contents

Introduction by the Chairman of the 2005 Convention

Scores of young people with Bibles in hand walking through the narrow streets of Keswick is my abiding memory of this year's convention. These young people, along with hundreds of chilidren and thousands of adults, all had the same purpose. We were in Keswick to seek to understand the content, true glory and life application of the gospel of God.

In this book we can only give a selection of the ministry given during the three weeks. However, every message given was recorded, so be sure to purchase a few tapes or CDs and benefit, as those present certainly did, from biblical and immensely practical ministry.

The ministry of Keswick continues to expand. The second Keswick in Zimbabwe is taking place as I write this introduction and discussions are also taking place regarding the launch of Keswick in Hungary.

A large team of volunteers make this convention possible and to them again, on behalf of the council, I want to give a huge thank you.

So, plan to join us all next summer when we will study together the subject of 'The Church in the Power of the Spirit.' I trust the material that follows will whet your spiritual appetite!!

Peter Maiden
Chairman Keswick Convention Council
October 2005

The Bible Readings

The Calling of Isaiah

by Stephen Gaukroger

STEPHEN GAUKROGER

Stephen is Senior Minister of Gold Hill Baptist Church in Buckinghamshire – the largest Baptist church in England. He is a prolific author, with a popular style, and his first book, *It makes sense,* has been used around the world to help people share their faith. He has been extensively involved in Christian initiatives in the UK, and until recently was on the Spring Harvest leadership team. He is on the Council of Spurgeon's College, was President of the Baptist Union of Great Britain from 1994 to 1995 and currently acts as a Consultant for the European board of the Luis Palau Evangelistic Association.

Stephen has a vision for a biblically literate Christian world and has particular concerns about the importance of the local church in the national scene, and the support and encouragement of local ministries. He is married to Janet, who is very involved with Christian work amongst the under-fives and worship. They have three children. He loves sport of all kinds!

L

The calling of Isaiah (1)

Isaiah 6

Introduction

It's a wonderful thing for a preacher at Keswick to have the privilege to take a whole week to expound a Bible book. I've chosen five chapters from Isaiah which I hope will give you the guts of an absolutely wonderful Old Testament book. I want to warn you that we'll have a fairly large amount of introductory material, setting the scene for the four days which are to follow.

Isaiah the man

There are three horizons in the book of Isaiah which will help us as we apply this. The first horizon is the personal; Isaiah himself. This man is clearly touched by God's almighty power. And what we're going to say must touch our lives as individuals. We will have to consider what it means for us as human beings, as husbands or wives, as people who are single or married, elderly or younger, in the workplace or already retired, our grand-parenting roles, our role as friends, as citizens, in the rigours and stresses of the workplace or whatever. Isaiah seems to have been born about 760 years before Jesus – some of this is conjecture but it fits broadly with what we understand of Old Testament history. I guess he's about twenty when this vision in

Isaiah 6 takes place. Then for forty years of prophetic ministry he shapes his religious community, until at least 701BC, which is the time we last know of him making significant prophetic utterances. Indeed, what he says goes far beyond to the nations of the world.

The material which we now know as Isaiah, from chapters 1 to 66, appears to have been collated in something like 680 or 690BC, when Isaiah would be about eighty years of age. But the book is not a detached ivory tower theologian's reflection on reality. It is a book in which Isaiah, as a man, is engaged and meeting with the living God. So that is the first horizon: we meet Isaiah. Do not allow the word of God to simply pass you by and not engage you as an individual.

The people of God

This is the second horizon. If you draw a line across the middle of what is sometimes known as the Holy Land, ten or so miles north of Jerusalem, and then go south down to places like Beersheba and so on, you are in the territory known as Judah. It encompasses the western bank of the Dead Sea and the Judean desert. It was in Judah, the southern kingdom, which included Bethany and Bethlehem, that Isaiah prophesied. The northern kingdom had long since split off from that in the south. It was in a separate entity altogether, still God's people but separated, known at this stage of Old Testament history as Israel. Isaiah is prophesying to the southern kingdom, the people of God gathered and clustered around the Jerusalem conurbation and further south, so the second horizon is the people of God. This book is addressed not just to individuals, it's not just about God transforming a man, Isaiah, but it's about God wanting to transform the covenant people of God.

The world

This is the third horizon. It is interesting that as Isaiah unfolds, the vista of his prophetic utterances is way beyond personal calls to repentance, although they exist. It is even beyond calls to the people of God to repent as a whole. Isaiah, particularly after chapter 40, has geopolitical implications for most of the ancient world. The Assyrians at least are in view and possibly other nations.

So what we'll hear will have personal consequences, covenant people consequences and global consequences, because that is the legitimate reach of the book of Isaiah. We must be careful not to read into this book things which aren't there but we must legitimately quarry away in this book to release what is there. Think personal, think covenant people, church, and think global.

Isaiah the book

There are sixty-six chapters in Isaiah. The name Isaiah means 'Yahweh' or 'God is salvation'. This is an evangelistic book, a salvation book, full of tales of God's deliverance. Now for 1,800 years of Christian history, pretty much everybody, apart from one Jewish writer and a Jewish writer that the first Jewish writer quotes, thought this book was a unity because it's come down to us as sixty-six chapters. Then in the middle of the 1800s a school of theology arose which began to have questions about the unity of the book, for two main reasons. One was because the linguistic style of chapters 39 to 55 and 55 to 66 seem very different from chapters 1 to 39, and the second was because there was antipathy to predictive prophecy. In other words, there was an unwillingness to believe that Isaiah could possibly be a prophetic operator rather than a political commentator. People felt that the chapters after 39, 40 following, could not have come from the pen of the same writer. So most serious scholars, for the last one hundred years, have believed that Isaiah was split into two or three sections, chapter 1 to 39 by Isaiah, chapters 39/40 to 55 by a second Isaiah and possibly chapters 55 to 66 by even a third Isaiah … Isaiah, the return of Isaiah, Isaiah strikes back.

We've got a number of problems with this view. One is that we have handed down to us, as a unity, sixty-six chapters in the book of Isaiah and we've got to find a way to work out how it all came together. Some people say there was a kind of Isaiah school of disciples who carried on his good work and kept writing bits and pieces in his name. I've always found that rather unconvincing. I think the linguistic difficulties can largely be explained by the difference in content and style. It's perfectly possible for one person to write and speak in a very different style in a completely different context. Many modern scholars have started to bring this argument full circle and most of the later commentaries, particularly by what are known as conservative evangelical scholars, have tended to re-argue for the unity of the whole book. My presupposition to you is this: the book of Isaiah was written by one person, Isaiah, of Jerusalem. He is responsible for all the content of chapters 1 to 66. He may have had an editorial role with some of it and pulled some chapters together but largely he was the overseer and deliverer and the vehicle that God used as a political prophetic commentator in the early chapters and a straightforwardly predictive prophetic commentator in the later chapters.

There is no book in the Bible with more predictive prophecy in it than Isaiah. There are at least 111 separate predictive instances in it. It is the third largest body of biblical truth in the entire Bible, after the Psalms and Jeremiah. And these 111 predictive statements are absolutely fundamental to the miraculous working of our God and I think the bottom line in this theological argument is this: 'Do we believe the Bible is a miraculous book?' If it is, it is capable of predictive prophecy; if it isn't then all bets are off. Once you say that, you've got some difficult questions to answer about the New Testament as well as the Old Testament.

The God of the Old Testament – different from the God of the New?

There's another misunderstanding about the Old Testament we need to address: that the Old Testament is full of wrath and anger and distance and transcendence and God being great and fantastic and the New Testament is about God being imminent and near and at hand in the person of Jesus. That's a caricature which cannot be sustained throughout the Old Testament. In Isaiah, early on in chapter 1:18, you see the prophet debunking that. '"Come now,"' 1:18 says, '"let us reason together," says the LORD. "Though your sins be as scarlet … they shall be as white as snow."' The deity of the universe, the God who created everything, is saying to sinful humanity, 'Come, let us reason together.' That is a remarkable statement in the Old Testament. It is encouraging human engagement. Yes, God is holy, God is magnificent, God is splendid. Yes, he lives in unexplored glory and splendour but he invites human engagement, even here in the Old Testament. 'Come, let us reason together.' 'I want to meet with you, and I want to talk with you. You're my people, I love you.' Even in the Old Testament, there is this kind of engagement. It's important for us to understand that God wants to speak to us. He is distant, he is holy, he is transcendent but he wants to speak.

Isaiah 6: the call of Isaiah

Let's come to this glorious calling that God brings to Isaiah. 'In the year that King Uzziah died' – this is Isaiah 6:1 – 'I saw the Lord high and exalted...' We're about to discover the most magnificent calling of someone to 'Christian ministry'. I use 'Christian ministry' in inverted commas; of course this is the Old Testament, but it's probably equally spectacular to the call of God in Acts to Paul, on the Damascus road. It's a dramatic calling to prophetic ministry.

Prophets were gathering strength during this period of Jewish history. 1 Samuel 9:9 is probably the first mention of a prophet being a 'seer' and the first pre-prophets are mentioned there. The prophetic ministry is gathering momentum during this phase. Isaiah is commissioned in the year that King Uzziah died. It's hard to date that. I think it's probably 740 or 742BC; nobody knows for sure but it's in that region. Uzziah was a reasonably good king and there was lots of stability during his reign – and when he died, as whenever a king died, there was enormous fear of turbulence and instability; political, economic and military. The safety of your life might be at stake until the new king became established, in the ancient world. This is a period of transition. Uzziah had been quite good as a king. He'd certainly allowed freedom for the prophets to operate and now he's dead, a new opportunity comes and God anoints Isaiah for service.

One reign ends but does God let his people loose with no voice? No: as one good thing ends another good thing is called into being by God. There are some lovely coincidences in church history. God takes one saint home and brings another one into the world. He never transitions his people without help and support. Uzziah dies and Isaiah is called to prophetic ministry: it's a very exciting time.

The nature of the vision: Isaiah 6:1-4

Isaiah was probably in the temple, although it's hard to know because it's a vision and so he may not physically be on the temple terrain. But he has this incredible vision – perhaps he's at worship in the temple – and he sees the Lord. It's a staggering thing to say. We're not sure what that means: is it the light, is it the sound? He may well have been overwhelmed by a sense of God being God. We're not entirely sure. The Bible says that no one can see God and live and there's a story about Moses seeing God and he sees 'the back parts' as God passes by. There's a great awe in the Old Testament about seeing God.

Somehow Isaiah is exposed to the magnificence of God in this vision. And 'the train of his robe' – even the NIV doesn't use language that helps us very much and we tend to use trains only of rail track or weddings. This is more like the wedding kind: it's this great glory flowing from him. Then in verse 2, above him were these seraphs, each with six wings. This is the only time in the Bible seraphs are mentioned in quite this way and we don't know what they were; they're obviously angelic beings with six wings.

The trouble is that we are very materialistic. Materialism can be used in two sort of senses: being a consumer and wanting things, and in a second sense, to mean being only concerned with that which you can see, touch and feel with the five senses. It's in that second sense that I mean it here. Isaiah was taken beyond the material. Presumably there are a variety of angelic beings; we know there are angels, archangels, seraphs, cherubim and various others. We don't know much about them, we just know there are heavenly beings. They are around in heavenly places. God is very creative and diverse in the human realm, isn't he? So it's reasonable to assume he's creative in the spiritual realm as well. There are a range of spirit beings, and we're not entirely sure what they are, but they do seem to be senior angels, magnificent, worshipping angels and they have all these wings and that's a symbol of glory.

They were calling to one another. This is actually about a liturgical worship session. They weren't just calling 'Hello!' to one another. This was what's called antiphonal worship and praise, as each eggs the other on to worship this great God. It was as if this side of the tent suddenly says, 'Crown him with many crowns' and the other side says 'The Lamb upon the throne!' Each side responds to the other side, louder and louder, encouraging each other in praise and worship. The seraphs say 'Holy' and the other ones say 'Holy' and the first ones say 'Holy is the Lord God Almighty!' They're egging one another on in praise and celebration.

Just as an aside, what a great thing the church would be if we egged one another on in praise and celebration, rather than gossip, criticism or destruction. Now some commentators have seen the first stirrings of the Trinity in this verse – 'Holy, holy, holy'. But even a commentator as erudite as John Calvin says they're stretching a point. It's really about the glory of God. This is actually a classic prophetic description. Sometimes the old translations translate it 'the Lord of hosts' – the phrase occurs twenty-five times in Malachi, for example. He's the Lord of the seraphs and the cherubim and the angels. He's the great Lord, the one calling Isaiah. 'The whole earth' (verse 3) – not just the heavenly places – 'is full of his glory.' At the sound of their voices (verse 4) the doorposts and thresholds shook and the temple is filled with smoke.

Isaiah's response: verses 5-7

This is a call like no other. This is a call of mind-shattering, mind-blowing extravagance. Isaiah would never be the same again. But notice what his response is to the glory of God (verse 5): '"Woe to me!" I cried. "I am ruined!"' The English translations find it very difficult to translate the word 'ruined' with enough vigour. It's hard to get the energy behind it. Some of us in pastoral ministry were trained to say things in a roundabout way: it's called circumlocution. We don't say some woman was being sinful, we say she was being rather less than she ought to have been. We can find a nice way of saying almost anything.

Isaiah is saying something fundamental here, and 'ruined' isn't strong enough. Probably the Hebrew is best understood as 'Woe is me.' There's an agony of soul here. He is saying 'For I am as good as dead! I am finished!' The word seems to imply non-existence: 'I am utterly broken from what I was.' The concept behind it is of utter devastation: 'I am absolutely ruined.' Notice he says 'For I am a man: unlike these seraphs, I'm not an angelic being, I'm just a human being, how can I cope with this (verse 5)? I'm not just a man, I am a man of unclean lips – a sinful man.' Then notice the incredible identification with the people of God. 'And I am from a people of unclean lips.' This is classic prophetic identification. You see it supremely, for example, in Nehemiah 1 and the prayers of Nehemiah 9 and Ezra 9 and so on. The prophets feel so burdened that they feel it for themselves, and in identification for the people of God.

The great tragedy of the church in Britain is that it is full of critics. It is easy for us to be condemnatory about churches, individually and corporately, and sometimes they need criticism but we must only do so if we can do so with loving identification with their sinfulness. Sometimes people talk about the church as if it belongs to somebody else. You know how you do this with your children? Am I the only one to do this? When they behave really well, when my son acts brilliantly in some dramatic part, I think, 'That's my boy!' When my middle daughter has a moment of hysteria I say, 'She's her mother's daughter.' Am I the only one to do that? Isaiah could easily have been destructive about the people of God. They were often in a mess but he chose to identify himself with their sinfulness: 'Woe is me! I am ruined! I am undone.'

The call of Isaiah is a great reminder that unless the glory of God results in a serious understanding of our own sinfulness, we probably haven't seen the glory of God at all. So much today that passes for spirituality in evangelical, spiritual, Bible-believing churches is a travesty of the glory of God. God is our friend in Jesus Christ but he is also the awesome Lord of the universe. Every time we seek to sweep our sin under the carpet and say 'It's not that bad, I just made a few mistakes,' we rob ourselves of genuine forgiveness. It's only when we see how great God is and we understand how poor we are in comparison that the glory of his grace can come flowing through to us. If you've done something you're ashamed of, to sweep it under the carpet will bring you peace for a moment but to bring it to God will bring you peace for a lifetime.

Here is the glory of the Lord filling the temple and he produces a sense of unbelievable uncleanness. Then there's this cauterising, this burning, cleansing experience. I've been reading this all my life and it's hardly ever occurred to me that a live coal placed on your lips hurts. It's probably never occurred to me until fairly recently because I've spiritualised it all the time. It was a painful experience – true repentance, true remorse, true sorrow for our sin can be painful but in the end it's worth it because you're called to greater glory.

Notice the seraph comes and, with an incredible hint of what's to come seven hundred years later, the sin is atoned for; it's dealt with. It points to the time when Jesus will be the great atoner for sin and there won't any more be the need for the sacrificial system or visions in the temple because it will all be centred on the atonement which Jesus Christ brings. Did Isaiah deserve this calling? No. Did he deserve forgiveness? No. It's this wonderful grace of God in his glory bringing forgiveness to Isaiah. I'm so moved by the story of John Newton, the slave-trader who messed his life up in so many ways and was part of the trade of human traffic. Slavery still exists today in some parts of the world: it's an obscenity to God that it should operate in such destructive malice in so many settings. John Newton, despite the rottenness in his soul and the abject misunderstanding of who God was, realised that he could be forgiven. He knew that he didn't deserve it at all. A slave-trader, a rebel against God, could suddenly see how great God was, be cleansed and know it was nothing to do with him and his goodness. And he could write the words 'Amazing grace, how sweet the sound, that saved a wretch like me.' A ruined wreck! 'I once was lost – undone – but now I'm found, was blind but now I see.' Fantastic, isn't it?

Isaiah's offer: verse 8

The great call of Isaiah in the glory of God results in a deep sense of sinfulness and ultimately, as he doesn't rush out of the temple, a great sense of cleansing. What a fantastic thing that is. What does salvation emanate from? A vision of the glory of God. A painful sense of guilt, and then a wonderful sense of forgiveness and, on the back of that salvation, what's the very first thing that God says to Isaiah? Having shown him how great he is, what's the next thing? He doesn't leave him in his wretchedness with theoretical forgiveness of sins in his mind; he calls him to something wonderful. 'Then I heard the voice of the Lord saying, "Who shall I send? And who will go for us?"' And you can hear Isaiah thinking to himself, you can't mean me! I'm unclean, I'm rotten, I'm a wretch, I've got nothing! And he says, 'I am willing to go. Here am I, send me.' And God said 'Go.' One of the wonderfully encouraging things about this for me is that having seen how wretched Isaiah is, he's still useful to God.

There isn't a person in this tent, however sinful, however far from God right now, who if we will see God in all his glory and repent, and turn from our sin, that God cannot use. God can use you today. He's that kind of God, whoever you are, if you'll come in repentance and faith. The old, the young, there's no retirement from God's service. You're not too old to be useful to him. The front page of one of the broadsheets this morning said 'Blair think tank is planning to increase the age of retirement to 67.' We're going to have to work longer and longer and longer to pay for our retirement, we really are going to have to do that. But in God's service there is no retirement. You're never too young – Paul told Timothy that – you're never too old. People in the Old Testament are used well into their eighties and beyond.

Isaiah's commission: verses 9–11

God says:

> Go and tell this people:'Be ever hearing, but never understanding;
> be ever seeing, but never perceiving.'

> Make the heart of this people calloused;
> make their ears dull
> and close their eyes.

Otherwise they might see with their eyes,
hear with their ears,
and understand with their hearts,
and turn and be healed.

Do you notice in your Bibles that these verses are inset slightly? That happens when it's poetry or a prophetic insight. And it's got what is technically called, verse 10, a chiastic structure. It's like this: look at verse 10: what is it that isn't working? Heart, ears, eyes: eyes, ears, heart – do you see how it goes in one direction like a big circle? It's a very Hebraic way of repeating something for emphasis. You tell them what you're going to tell them, you tell them and you tell them what you've told them. At the General Election before last, Tony Blair said he'd got three priorities – education, education, education. This is a Hebraic way of emphasising something. It's quite a common technique in the Old Testament.

Verse 11:

Then I said, 'For how long, O Lord?'
And he answered:
'Until the cities lie ruined
and without inhabitant,
until the houses are left deserted
and the fields ruined and ravaged,
until the LORD has sent everyone far away
and the land is utterly forsaken.
And though a tenth remains in the land,
it will again be laid waste.'

Then there's a very obscure thing about terebinth and oak, which may be two kinds of oak trees, no one's entirely sure, they 'leave stumps when they are cut down, so the holy seed will be the stump in the land.' There'll be devastation and ruin and this prophecy was completely fulfilled, but there will be a stump left in the ground – a sign of hope.

What a call! 'Isaiah, go and tell the people to repent and turn to me, and by the way, they won't.' The prophets were always miserable. They were never satisfied. Jonah went to Nineveh and preached to the Ninevites and they repented and he was not happy. Isaiah went to preach to the Judeans and they didn't repent and he wasn't happy. God said to him, 'Preach to them but they're not going to respond.' God knew, in his sad foreknowledge in this particular case, the human heart was going for a long time yet to be resistant until the stump (possibly a continuing hint of Jesse's rod, a descendent of David) is ultimately fulfilled in Jesus Christ: until that point they're not going to 'get it' and respond to the incredible good news.

Pray for revival: prepare for exile

I think this is enormously prescient for our culture today in 2005. My own view is that we are going to preach and preach the word but it may be that we have to wait a while before people turn in repentance to the living God. We should pray for revival but prepare for exile. If God brings revival next month to Great Britain, it will be thrilling. If God brings it, hallelujah. We must work for revival and pray for it, and share our faith with passion and energy but we may have to prepare for a period of exile. And we may have to be ready for the centre of gravity of the church to shift to the Third World, where it's growing rapidly. We may have to learn to live in exile as the people of God. God may be stripping away the flabby mediocrity of much of our church life until yet again we come to the temple for a vision of the holy, almighty and living God. We may preach and they may not hear and they may not respond in repentance and they may not understand. Many will. This is not an excuse, by the way, for a kind of remnant-itis. You know how some people are in their churches: 'There are only six of us now in our church left. We must be doing something right! All those other compromising churches down the road that are growing ... no, we holy ones ...' Don't get remnant-itis.

We may be facing this massive challenge. People may not respond, they may not hear but God will not leave himself without a stump of an oak, without a remnant of a witness, without people who love him, who want to serve him, who will want to respond to the call of Christ as Jesus issued it to the disciples centuries later. 'Go into all the world and preach the gospel' is an echo of this passage in Isaiah chapter 6.

I want you to focus in these closing moments on the personal horizon, on the Isaiah who had his guilt atoned for by the glorious grace of God and I'd like you to reflect on the amazing grace of God in the cleansing call that came to Isaiah. Don't miss the splendour of the temple, the fear that came into Isaiah because of his sinfulness, the wonder of his forgiveness, the greatness of his calling and the impossibility of his task because people were not going to respond posi- tively. In the end that was God's business and not Isaiah's business. He's looking for a church, a covenant people who will yet again seek his face, who will yet again be obedient, whatever the response, and who will view their glorious calling of God as being absolutely central to who they are.

The good news and the bad news (2)

Isaiah chapter 9

Introduction

This is about a wonderful future. It's going to be pretty dark and difficult before it's wonderful and so we'll need to hang in there. The
material yesterday and the material today is the hardest of the week.
The chapters for the final three days are actually much easier to get to
grips with than these opening chapters and their complexities. This
material is particularly convoluted and difficult because we are at that
section now where Isaiah is not just prophesying but predicting and
whenever those two ideas are conflated, forth-telling and fore-telling,
it becomes quite tricky. We talked yesterday about the three horizons
of application: the geo-political or the global; the covenant people and
the church; and the personal. Prophecy itself has a number of horizons which again are quite tricky to discern. The prophetic horizons
of the prophets are, firstly, the immediate future. God's judgement will
fall, the Assyrians will come and the exile will begin. These are
prophecies of a relatively immediate application. Then there are what
might be called 'messianic' prophecies, which have a slightly further
timeframe, looking to the first century when Jesus the Saviour of the
world was born. Finally, even further on, some of the prophecies are
about the second coming of Jesus Christ and so are not yet fulfilled.

We live today stranded between the 'now' and the 'not yet' of biblical fulfilment. That's what we have here; a relatively immediate fulfilment assigned to the original people, a looking forward to a messianic age when Jesus will come in the first century and a hint that even then it's not all fulfilled. There is a future, a second coming, a wrapping up of all of global history to be looked forward to. So there are a variety of horizons and that is what makes much of this material complicated.

Identification: Isaiah 8

Notice firstly how Isaiah identifies himself so fully with the message – this is quite an important feature for us. We live in a world today in which talk is cheap. People say things easily, and I hear Christians all the time using the right words. They are sound theologically, they sing the right songs, they may even have expressions of praise and worship that look very holy but their lives don't add up with what they sing. That dislocation between life and lip is a huge problem for the church today. It was a great problem in Isaiah's day – they rarely neglected temple worship but they regularly neglected the worship of God. We could be sitting here perfectly happily, singing the songs and listening to the Bible teaching, but we could just as easily walk from this tent and commit an act of gross sinfulness and some of us would see no conflict at all between what we'd said and what we were about to do.

That disjunct between life and behaviour is the opposite of the Isaiah we read about. Isaiah is so much the embodiment of his message that even his children are named in order to embody this message. 'The LORD said' (this is chapter 8:1) 'take a large scroll and write on it with an ordinary pen, naming your first child.' I believe that this is the longest name given to a baby in the Old Testament: Maher-Shalal-Hash-Baz. It's quite significant: Isaiah so owns the prophetic burden which the living God has given him that even his family relationships are drawn into that prophetic utterance. Worship, experienced ecstatically, which it must have been in Isaiah 6 in the temple, works itself out in life. And that link between worship and life is fundamental. Indeed the New Testament word for worship doesn't imply a distinction between what you do on a Sunday and what you might do on a Monday. There's no distinction; it's about all of life.

There's been a lovely token this morning for me actually. John could not have known the significance of the hymn he chose a few moments ago, 'I cannot tell whom He who angels worship'... That hymn has been sung at my wedding, my ordination, my induction to my first church and my induction to the church where I'm now pastor. For me, there was something amazing about that great call at the end 'at last the Saviour of the world is king'. My whole ministry has been geared to telling people about that king and the worship and my life came together this morning in a quite remarkable way. Worship and life must not be in any way ripped apart.

Here's Isaiah, he owns what he is about to say and he is so passion-ate about this reality that he wants the people of God to understand what he understands. He's not after them aping the experience he had. There isn't a hint in Isaiah that he wants them to experience the same experience he had of the vision of God in the temple. He's not inter-ested in the replication of an experience: he simply wants them to meet the same God and be transformed by him in whatever way that God, Yahweh, chooses to reveal himself to his people. So in chapter 8, which is the lead-up to chapter 9, Isaiah is desperate for people to con-sult God, to listen to him. And this is where this material gets compli-cated because not only is it hard to get people to concentrate and to focus and to seek God, but the material is all interwoven; the political, the Assyrians make an appearance, the Philistines make an appearance, the northern kingdom makes an appearance, the southern kingdom makes an appearance, Isaiah himself makes an appearance, the prophetic horizons all make an appearance. It's incredibly difficult to unravel. Understanding this passage is completely impossible without the help of the Holy Spirit, to guide us and to direct us in this work.

Look at verse 18 because this is the context of that fantastic passage we read in Isaiah 9. 'Here am I' – he's already said this in chapter 6, he's told God he's available, 'and the children the LORD has given me' – my whole family are available to you, God. 'We are signs and symbols' – that's going to come up in a quite significant way in a moment. 'We are signs and symbols in Israel from the LORD Almighty, who dwells in Zion.' 'So I and my family are signs to this nation because we are sold out to the living God. We've heard from him, we seek him, and we want you to seek him too.'

Looking in the wrong place: Isaiah 8:19

The immediate context, both before and after these verses, is of the people who seek in the wrong place or who don't seek God at all. Verse 19: 'When men tell you to consult mediums and spiritists, who whisper and mutter, should not a people enquire of their God? Why consult the dead on behalf of the living?' The words 'whisper' and 'mutter' mean that when you went to visit a necromancer, someone who consulted the dead, it was in a darkened room with a little whispering going on. This is contrasted with the prophetic word of Yahweh which was absolutely clear, in broad daylight and available for people to hear.

Why consult the dead on behalf of the living? The Old Testament is crystal clear that this kind of spiritism is wholly alien to God's plan for human beings. It's sickeningly opposed to the seeking of the one true God. But, Isaiah said, 'We are supposedly God's covenant people but we've fallen so far from seeking him that though we're desperate, our culture broken, though wickedness abounds, though we're shattered as a community, we go on seeking spirit mediums, consulting the dead on behalf of the living. No wonder we're in such a mess.'

By the way, the problem here is not that they'd stopped worshipping Yahweh and started being spiritualists, in the sense we might understand it. It's they'd become syncretists, which means that they had no problem at all in worshipping Yahweh, a little nod in his direction, but at the same time they had no problem at all in seeking the advice of the dead, in direct contradiction to Scripture. This is classically the problem of the early third millennium in which we live. Very few people reject Christianity out of hand if you push them, but they'll say 'That's fine, if that's what you want to believe.' They have that patronising view of it. More and more people are perfectly happy to dribble along with a bit of faith and to pray in a crisis but everything else is up for grabs: tolerance is king. Everything works. At the heart of a society in decay, here in the 700s BC and at the heart of our society, is a society that doesn't know who to turn to. And Isaiah says you must turn and enquire of the Lord. But because we enquire of any human wisdom and occultic powers and anybody else, even today, we are not getting what we need to get from God because we're enquiring in all the wrong places.

It's bizarre. People consult their horoscopes, not just simply as a bit of fun but seriously to see the guidance they need for their lives. Some months ago I compared the horoscopes in a number of daily papers. I looked up the same star sign in two different papers. On one day this occultic influence said 'Today's a day to take care. Put decisions of a major nature off until tomorrow.' But in the next paper it said 'Today is a day for bold action.' Very confusing. Isaiah says 'Enquire of the Lord, not in occultic and dark powers and not from anybody else apart from him.' To the law and to the testimony, go to them. They will guide you and they will keep you.

Disaster: Isaiah 8:22-9:1, 9:8-15

The introduction to chapter 9, the last verse of chapter 8, refers to 'distress and darkness … fearful gloom'. Then chapter 9 emerges into some light; 'There will be no more gloom for those who were in distress. In the past he humbled Zebulun and Naphtali'… Isaiah looks back probably to around the 730s BC when Tiglath-Pileser came down and roughed up significant number of these tribes and left them devastated, crushed almost beyond recognition.

Let's just move past the good news for a moment and get to verse 8, because this chapter is understood surrounded by bad news. 'The LORD has sent a message against Jacob; it will fall on Israel.' This is a prophecy to the northern kingdom as well as the southern kingdom. 'All the people will know it – Ephraim and the inhabitants of Samaria – who say with pride' (verse 9)…This is the key to not hearing from God personally – pride. The children of Israel were filled with pride. 'We'll do what we want, we'll kill the prophets, we'll ignore God's messengers, we'll do it our way.' Sound familiar? Pride is almost always national pride and personal pride is nearly always the cause of disaster. We're not humble enough to seek God.

Look at these proud northerners: 'The bricks have fallen down' – we've been defeated 'but we will replace those bricks with dressed stone' (verse 10). 'Tiglath-Pileser may have knocked down our little terrace but we're going to rebuild a very nice three-bedroom semi. We're not at all intimidated by this. We're going to build even better.' 'The fig-trees have been felled, but we will replace them with cedars' (verse 10). 'We're going to have our garden completely landscaped, never mind the mess. We don't need your help, thank you; we will sort all this out.' But, verse 11 says, they can't, because 'the Lord has strengthened' their enemies. The Arameans are coming from the east, the Philistines from the west and they're going to eat them up. And 'Yet for all this, his anger is not turned away, his hand is still upraised' (verse 12). His people haven't returned to him, 'nor have they sought the LORD Almighty' (verse 13). Then Isaiah identifies two of the causes of this great wickedness. 'The LORD will cut off from Israel, both head and tail, both palm branch and reed in a single day' (verse 14) and then he describes what he means by that so that we're not left in any doubt: 'The elders and prominent men are the head, and the prophets who teach lies are the tail' (verse 15).

Leadership in danger

Lying prophets are the abomination of the Old Testament. There's that great story where one of the kings calls in a faithful prophet and says 'Shall I go to war?' and the prophet says 'You will and you'll win.' The king's angry and says 'No, tell me the truth.' And the prophet says words to the effect of 'I tell you the truth and you don't listen. The truth is, you can go to war but you'll be killed.' And he goes to war and he is.

Lying prophets; there were quite a lot of them about. There were some honest, good ones as well. What's the problem with Israel in the north, and Judah in the south? Fundamentally these people are wicked and sinful. The fatherless, widows, orphans, they're all implicated, as the chapter goes on to tell us, but Isaiah lays much of the blame at the foot of leadership: elders who had both a political and a religious significance and prophets who had a slightly-outside-the-institution authority. You couldn't trust the leaders to say the right thing and even those who are supposed to speak for God were lying and offering comforting words where there were no comforting words to be offered. So Isaiah says, 'It's an absolute mess because leaders have failed God's people.'

What an amazing challenge it is to be a leader in God's church. Whatever our role in leadership is, God has tasked us with integrity of life and honesty of purpose. Leadership is often blamed in the Bible when it runs away from God. It can't be perfect, because only Jesus was perfect, and leadership can only do what it can do. Sometimes it can't lead if people won't follow. But in the end if God has called us to leadership, there is huge weight on our shoulders. It's not a weight we should bear alone: we should bear it in the power of the Holy Spirit, but nevertheless there's a challenge to integrity in leadership. I cannot remember a time in my ministry when I was more aware of the sinful failings of leaders. If the flock of God are not led clearly, just as in Isaiah's time, then the church of God is bound to be led into a cul-de-sac. We must pray for godly leaders to be raised up; prophets who tell the truth, people who preach the word, who are unwilling to compromise, even when it's painful.

Leadership is a wonderful thing. Lots of people want to be leaders

> I want to be a leader
> When great success gives fame
> But I'm not so keen
> When a failing's seen
> And they're looking for someone to blame.

When everything's going well, isn't it great? I listen to pastors talk about their churches. When they're growing, they talk about 'my church'. 'My church is doing really well.' When the church is failing and declining in numbers, they say 'Those people at the church …' Leadership's a challenge here. Isaiah needed rather more support than he got. Pray for your leaders. Pray for them regularly, care for them and love them as they face the challenges of leading the church into the future. There are two sides; sometimes it's the people of God who need to be prayed for as much as those who lead them.

Isaiah is absolutely adamant that ungodly leadership has contributed to this great horror. Verse 17, the Lord won't take pleasure in the young men, he can't even pity the fatherless and widows: everyone's ungodly! Verse 18, 'Surely wickedness burns like a fire' – it consumes everything like a forest fire. Verse 19: the wrath of the Lord Almighty is coming. And yet his anger is still not turned away. This was a land in turmoil, kings came and kings went but the worship of the living God was neglected. The temple was still there physically and probably people still went to it but the passion, the faith, the all-consuming life of God, which Isaiah knew, was apparently nowhere to be seen. The infrastructure had been broken down by successive invading armies. Stones were piled where houses once stood. The waterways which provided irrigation for the crops were dirtied so the fields lay empty. Security was minimal; warfare was common. Thuggery was everywhere; it was a society that was increasingly decaying.

Sometimes, as Christians get older, we think things have never been as bad as they are now. It is true, in the last one hundred years in Britain, there's been a huge abandonment of the core principles of the Ten Commandments. But the world has been very, very bad before. The trouble is, as you get older, it gets harder and harder to accept that, because you view the past through rose-coloured, nostalgic spectacles.

When I was a young minister, I was thrilled to introduce change and energy and life, and now sometimes young people come and say 'Do you think we could do this?' I think, cheeky young pups! When I was young I was ready for revolution and revival, let's change everything! What was wrong with this wretched Christian establishment? Why weren't they more flexible, more adaptable, more change-orientated? Now here I am, part of that boring establishment. Things have often been bad in the past. Things were terrible in Isaiah's day and things are bad today, from a Christian point of view, in the western world. But the same hope is present and it's encapsulated in this Christmas reading.

The good news: Isaiah 9:2-5

The centrepiece of Isaiah 9, these early verses, gives hope and light to all this unremitting gloom. 'The people walking in darkness have seen a great light.' Sometimes the Hebrew uses a tense which is called the prophetic perfect. It implies an event has occurred when it's actually still to occur and it does so in order to guarantee its certainty. It's important because this is a looking forward section to these various prophetic horizons. They've seen a great light and 'on those living in the land of the shadow of death a light has dawned'. Recognise this phrase from Psalm 23: 'though I walk through the valley of the shadow of death'? It's quite an unusual Old Testament phrase and doesn't occur that often. Then Isaiah talks about the enlarging of the nation, which is shrinking. The people look back to David's day when the traditional limits of the land, Dan in the north and Beersheba in the south, were far extended. David presided over an empire far larger than that. This king is coming whose borders will be extended way beyond the borders that they naturally understand to be their rightful land. And they'll be rejoicing, just like they do when they divide up pillage and plunder and Midian, the great enemy, will be defeated.

The day will come when all the bloody accoutrements of war, verse 5, will be dealt with, wrapped up, finished, settled, because the answer to this brutal oppression, to societal decay, to personal religious sloppiness and even religious sin, is going to be a child.

The Christ: Isaiah 9:6-7

A male child will be born. 'And the government will be on his shoulders.' Literally, that means the government will be his responsibility. He'll exercise governance. Then his forenames are given. These names are wonderfully exciting and they're truer now than when Isaiah uttered them. 'He will be called Wonderful Counsellor.' The King James version has two words there, 'And he shall be called Wonderful, Counsellor'. The newer translations run them together and say they're just four couplets: Wonderful Counsellor, Mighty God, Everlasting Father and Prince of Peace. Is it two words or one phrase? The answer is 'Yes.' We simply don't know. They're nouns and they could stand alone but they're also wonderfully paired, for reasons that the rest of the context seems to make clear. He will be a wonderful counsellor; the word 'wonderful' is only ever used of God's activity in the Old Testament. It's never used of man's wonderful activity. Solomon is described as having wonderful wisdom but it's a different word. David is described as having wonderful military power but it's a different word. Only God is described in this way.

A son is coming, a child will be born, says Isaiah; you won't see it fully in your generation. Ahaz, who'd asked for a sign, is going to get one. Isaiah 7:14 gives a hint of what this sign will be: 'Therefore the LORD himself will give you a sign: The virgin will be with child and will give birth to a son, and will call him Immanuel.' Micah, Isaiah's contemporary, says in chapter 5:2 that it's in Bethlehem where this Messiah will emerge to do his work.

Isaiah's saying, he'll be a wonderful counsellor, counsellor to kings. He'll be a guidance to the nation. What did the nation of Israel need? It needed godly counsel to put it in the right direction. What do we need, most of us? We need a wonderful counsellor and he's arrived! The prophetic dimension has come; not the complete one but the middle one – the Jesus event in Bethlehem two thousand years ago. The wonderful counsellor is now available to us. He's available to our churches and to our nation, so why don't we enquire of him?

It's symbolic and significant that it's a child, because it's not by military might. The great Saviour of the world rode not a stallion but a donkey into Jerusalem. This passage is about humility: God comes not shaking his fist, demonstrating all his power in some arrogant way. He's a child, and even as a child there's more power in the little finger of the newborn Christ child than there's ever been anywhere on earth at any phase, ever.

The Christ child is the wonderful counsellor. And he's the mighty God. He might be a child but he is mighty and he is God. Isaiah's saying to the people, no human solution will do it for us, we're never going to get the military might together to defeat Tiglath-Pileser and his hordes, it's not going to happen! Sennacherib's going to come, we're not strong enough! We're a little group; we can't do it! When in

597, and then again in 587, the Babylonians come and Nebuchadnezzar whisks everybody away to Babylon, seventy years will have to elapse before Nehemiah and Ezra and others bring the people back to the Promised Land. How does that happen? Does it happen because they suddenly discover an incredible leader, a Nebuchadnezzar, an Alexander the Great? No. It's because they have a mighty God.

A mighty God: verse 6

We are not going to take our nation by storm. Our churches aren't going to suddenly rise up in revival power, making a difference in the towns where we are, because we are all brilliant. But we have a mighty God. Isaiah has to convince us that we have a mighty God. He's huge. He's bigger than our imagination. He is the God of the universe. He's so powerful he didn't need to flex his muscles in some military way – he could be born as a baby. And forever after that the Christ child could bring deliverance and victory and hope and life.

He is the everlasting Father, which seems a bit confusing. How can a child be a father? It's because Isaiah's trying to tell us that this child will be utterly and absolutely identified with the fatherhood of God. This would have sounded obscene and blasphemous to many Jews. Do you remember Jesus getting into terrible trouble with the Pharisees because he said 'I am'? He used the name of God for himself and they went wild. How can this man do it? Do you remember the story about the four men digging a hole through the roof? They let a man on a bed down and Jesus, seeing their faith, heals him and then says, 'Your sins are forgiven.' What shocks the crowd the most? Not so much the physical healing, although that's amazing. Who is this, they say, who can forgive sin? They're staggered by his revelation of his divinity. He is the mighty God, the everlasting Father, he's identified with the Father. God has always been Father and Jesus has always existed.

Because God is the Everlasting Father, we know that Jesus wasn't born. He always existed in eternity with God, because God has always been called Father. If Jesus had had to be born at some point there would have been a point before which God wasn't Father, because he hadn't been the father of Jesus. Fatherhood is a derivative from manhood. I've always been male and at some point I became a father, because my children were born. Before my children were born, I was still a man. God has always been a father, he's everlastingly the Father, and if he was everlastingly the Father he must have everlastingly have had a Son. And because he's everlastingly had a Son, Jesus is eternal, God is eternal, and together they are eternally reigning and ruling. Isaiah, in his wonderful prophetic insight, wraps it all up together and says, 'A baby's going to be born and he'll have all these God-like qualities because he's going to be God. And it's going to be totally mysterious because a virgin will conceive and give birth (Is. 7:14). It won't just be any baby, it'll be a God baby.'

All babies are special but there is a baby prophesied years before, who has come into the world and the world will never be the same again. This baby divides all of history into before he came and after he came. And he isn't finished yet. Because he's not only these things, he is the Prince of Peace and 'of the increase of his government and peace there will be no end'. At the end of Isaiah 9 you read about Manasseh and Ephraim fighting each other. God's come to bring peace between family members who war against each other. He's come to bring peace between nations. He's come to bring peace to the planet. But it hasn't happened yet. We are now in the third prophetic horizon – peace hasn't come to the world, bloodshed is everywhere, it may even increase. Has the Prince of Peace not come? Of course he's come, he's bringing peace now as a sign into the life of every man and woman who will receive him, by faith with repentance, as Saviour and Lord. The Prince of Peace will come to any human being who in desperation and openness comes to him and receives him.

One day the Prince of Peace, the Christ child, the virgin baby, long promised, will come back and his peace will reign over the earth. And every garment rolled in blood will be put on the fire. Swords will be beaten into ploughshares: all weapons destroyed, hunger and pain gone, every tear wiped away from our eyes. Our future is assured because the Christ child came, because we put our trust in him. The future of the planet is not in the hands of the United Nations, nor any super power. The government will be on his shoulders. Jesus is in control of history. Our destiny is inextricably linked with the destiny of the Son of God. He is the Prince of Peace. He is the Everlasting Father, he is the Mighty God, he is the one who will re-envision and re-empower us as we worship and adore the Christ child.

It's a great God (3)

Isaiah chapter 40

Introduction

In chapters 39 and 40, the scene shifts, the prophetic horizon has moved. The early chapters (broadly chapters 1-39), although they contain some long-range prophecies about the Messiah's coming, are rooted largely in the period from 740BC, when Isaiah is called, to 701BC when Hezekiah and Sennacherib are having their arguments. The scene now shifts 150 years to the end of exilic period. During the 600s, the people of God were serially attacked and not attacked and were a bit stronger and a bit weaker until, in around 597BC, the invading Babylonian army came and whisked away captives. Ten years later, not having done a complete job, in 587BC further captives were taken away to the land of Babylon, and the book of Daniel deals with this.

Towards the end of the Babylonian captivity, which lasted about seventy years, characters such as Nehemiah and Ezra, Haggai and others appear and the children of Israel dribble back from exile into the Promised Land. These words of comfort in Isaiah 40 come as a prophetic utterance, spoken in the 700s, for specific help to the people of God in the 500s, some 150 years later. They are in desperate need of the courage to step out from under the oppression of the

Medeo-Persian empire and to regain the promised land of Jerusalem, which was, by rights, theirs to possess.

'It is a great God' is the theme this morning. In Isaiah 40:1-9 we have the God of rescue, in Isaiah 40:10-26 we have the God without equal, and then in verses 27-31, we have the God of hope. These three points will help us unpack this very significant passage.

The God of Rescue: Isaiah 40:1-9

What is not clear in your English Bible is that 'Comfort my people' is a particularly technical Hebrew part of speech. These are imperatives, a command. 'I am now telling you,' says God, 'that the period of what is known as duress will come to an end and the people of God will know comfort and freedom.' The tough time they have been through – what the NIV translated as hard service, literally period of oppression – is over. These imperatives, because these are plurals, are either calling the heavenly hosts in angelic array to marshal all of their forces to bring comfort in great measure to the people of God, or it is plural because it is appealing to Isaiah and perhaps Micah and others who were Isaiah's contemporaries, the whole prophetic school, anyone who will listen who speaks for God. It is saying 'All of you together, raise your voices and cry now is the time for comfort, now is the time for deliverance, now is the time when the people of God's duress, their hard service will come to an end and they will know comfort and freedom.' This is very good news in a very bad news book. I can't say that Isaiah is totally full of bad news but there is a fair amount of judgement.

The children of Israel are coming to an end of this exilic period, this grotesque persecution. The story of Daniel is well known to us. Continually through this great man's period of service he experiences the persecution of an oppressive regime. He is symbolic of what all the people of God endure: thrown into a lions' den for daring to pray and defying the king's edict. Three of his friends are thrown into a fiery furnace for refusing to acknowledge an idol, made by an arrogant king. They have been ripped from their comfort zones in Jerusalem; the godly implements have been taken from the temple; the nation vanquished and now they are under the authority of a plethora of gods, none of which they recognise or own. And at the end of this grinding persecution and this horrific exile, as it drifts towards an end, they are broken, disillusioned and fed up. They have hardly got the emotional energy to respond to the prophetic word of God.

God mobilises the prophetic forces and the hosts of heaven and says 'Comfort my people, wrap them around with my arms of love.' Then verse 3, which is taken on board by John the Baptist, as the announcer of Jesus, verse 3, 'I am the voice of one calling in the desert, make straight in the wilderness a highway for our God.' God is saying, 'I am going to make it possible for you to get back every mountain range that you believe you can't cross on this journey. It will be as it were level to your feet, every deep valley will be levelled out.'

The road home

The journey from Babylon to Jerusalem was a nine-hundred mile, four month enterprise – it was no mere Sunday afternoon picnic stroll. It was a huge undertaking. Initially a few stragglers returned, facing warring tribes along the way, people perfectly ready to murder for a small amount of loot or even clothing. That trickle was to become a stream, and the stream a flood, as the children of Israel made their almost one thousand mile journey back to the Promised Land. God says 'Comfort my people with this thought, that as they set off, I will be bulldozing mountains metaphorically and levelling valleys and making the way straight and I will blaze a trail for them.' No wonder John the Baptist takes this prophecy for himself, as he sees himself blazing a trail for Jesus in the first century, knocking down things. The axe is laid to the roots, John the Baptist says, clearing the way, getting the forest level, making a path for the Messiah to come, just as in Isaiah God makes a path for the people of God to come (Lk. 3:9).

A God of rescue: there will be those in this tent who feel as though they have been in captivity for a very long time. Their workplace feels oppressive, their marriage or family life is difficult, they are worried about their children, concerned for their parents, or they are struggling with emotional turbulence and the anxiety of mental illness or psychological stress. Many of God's people feel weary beyond recognition. And these people were without hope; brutalised for so long, they have hardly got the energy to get up and make it back to the Promised Land. They have been in an oppressive situation for so long, they simply haven't got the strength to rise up and take all that God has promised for them.

The church of Jesus sometimes feels like that. Thank God for the growth of the church in so many places around the world. Sadly, very few of those dramatic events are taking place in the western advanced so-called First World. It makes me wonder, when God is so at work in what is called the Third World, and so apparently not at work in what is called the First world, whether we have any right to think of ourselves as the First World at all. We feel bound, our churches feel small and ineffective, very often. Is there any hope?

The Lord comes to this tent and for you in your situation, wraps his loving arms of comfort around you and wants you to know his affirmation, his strength. He will go before you, he will go back before you, he will blaze a trail back to where you live and when you get back home you will find he is there already, waiting for you with renewal, restoration and strength, if you will come to him. Some of us have lived in the foreign land too long, we have been in the wilderness far too long, we have been too long away from God and he calls us back to himself. Make the journey back. It may not be nine hundred miles, it may be the journey of a split second, as we repent and follow him.

'Comfort my people' – why? Because I am going to make it possible. 'All men are like grass', verse 6 says, 'their glory fades, the grass withers and the breath of God blows it away but the word of our God stands forever.' So of course we don't have the strength on our own – we are like grass, the Bible says, but the word of the Lord abides for ever. God is good. God is the God of comfort and God is the God of strength. Look at verse 9 – which is what I sometimes call a Janus verse[1], because it transitions between the God of rescue and the God

---

[1] Janus was the Roman god who faced both ways, looking into the past and the future.

without equal. This verse looks back to the God of rescue and forwards to what will be a poem of praise to the God without equal. It is a pivotal verse. 'You who bring good tidings to Zion' ... to Jerusalem, you bring this good tidings from Babylon ... 'go up on a high mountain ... lift up your voice with a shout ... say to the towns of Judah (as you approach Jerusalem) don't be afraid ... "Here is your God ... who comforts you."'

We're getting nearer, the towns of Judah are appearing, they are nearly back home. How many of you have ever travelled anywhere with young children? 'Are we nearly there yet?' Ours occasionally ask that before we even get out of the drive. What a palaver it is getting one family ready to get out but there is a whole nation to get ready to get out of Babylon. Imagine trying to get thousands of people back from Babylon. It's an absolute mess. And as they get nearer and nearer, imagine the excitement. And here's comfort for you: you're not nine hundred miles from home, you're not four months from home, you are a change of heart and mind and a prayer away from home. That can happen in a moment. It is not without cost – it demands a change of life, of commitment, but God is waiting to comfort his people. How? Because God is not only a God of rescue. Verse 9 transitions us into the God without equal.

To whom will you compare God? Verses 10–26

In these verses, Isaiah systematically sets out to to dismantle all the rivals to the living God. He dismantles all opposition, every rival, every pretender to the divine throne. The situations into which Isaiah prophesies – early 700BC and the middle of the 500s BC – are polytheistic and syncretistic. That is very important. They are not atheistic. In the ancient world there were almost no atheists. It was very, very unusual. The kind of atheism you meet today – 'I don't believe in God' – was very, very rare in the ancient world. The problem wasn't atheism. Psalm 14 says rather mockingly 'the fool has said in his heart there is no God' and this is one of the very rare Old Testament references to anything remotely atheistic, because only an idiot would say there isn't a God.

When I travel in certain countries, particularly countries of a Muslim nature, I find it much easier to talk about God than I do here. They have no problem at all in talking about God. I was in a Middle Eastern country for four or five days, doing some work, staying in a hotel, and it wasn't safe for me to drive myself so I was assigned a driver. The driver was from Pakistan and he was a Muslim. He drove me everywhere and we got an opportunity to talk. He told me about his family and he was continually talking to me about God. It was no problem at all. 'Why are you here?' 'I'm a Christian.' It was no problem to talk about God to an ordinary Muslim. Try talking to an ordinary person in Britain about God and you get funny looks.

That was the culture in the ancient world. It was polytheistic; there were loads of gods, all at the same time and all muddled in together. The Roman times were like that: Jesus entered a world of the same kind of polytheism. It wouldn't have worried the Roman powers one jot if the disciples said 'Jesus is God.' The Romans would have said 'Great, come on, let's have him in with the rest of them, one more god, what's that to us?' But the early Christians said, 'He's the only one who's God.' It was their intolerance of religious tolerance that made the early Christians so hated. If you want to know what is going to make us hated in Britain in the next ten years, I promise you it is this. Try telling people that Jesus is the only way to God. I promise you that intolerance will cause you trouble in the coming years, as litigation develops, as our laws are changed, as the war on terror continues to make us more and more sensitive, and we try to pass more and more laws to accomplish what only God's Spirit can.

So into this polytheistic, multi-god, multi-faith world, Isaiah comes and says 'Now listen, I am going now to assure you, as you get ready to come home, that your God is the God without equal, that he is the only God, and that he is going to systematically get rid of all the other pretenders.' Who will we compare God with? Comparison is everything. Are you a nice person? Compared with whom? That's important. Who shall I compare you with? This is a big congregation. Compared with what? Compared with some of the churches of Korea or Southeast Asia this is a Sunday school class. Compared with your church, it is a reasonable size. Everything is about comparison. I often find this in witnessing. You talk to someone about coming to know Jesus and they say, 'I'm as good as the next person.' So Isaiah deconstructs the enemies.

God of loving comfort

Verse 10 – 'The sovereign LORD comes with power, and his arm rules for him.' As we are just about to get into power metaphors, it suddenly ends up feeling like Psalm 23 and John 10. 'He tends his flock like a shepherd, he gathers the lambs in his arms. He carries them close to his heart; he gently leads those who have young.' God is a God without equal because he is a God who is present in loving comfort. There are a lot of lies going round about the Old Testament; that the Old Testament is about transcendence, and God being great, and the New Testament is about immanence, and God being present in the person of Jesus. There are elements of truth in that but you cannot wish for a more tender image than this of God. Yes, he's holy, yes, he's distant, yes, he's sovereign, but he wraps his children up like a tender shepherd looking after young lambs. Are you feeling fearful of a holy God? You should. But he is not only holy, he is a shepherd who loves to wrap you and me in his arms.

No other ancient god was like this. The Baals that Elijah was so fond of mocking – do you think there was the slightest tenderness about them? No. This God is both transcendent and shepherd-like, and notice verse 12 tells us that he is Lord of creation. 'Who has measured the waters in the hollow of his hand?' Now I know what you are saying – isn't this a bit anthropomorphic? Anthropomorphism is simply when you attribute to God characteristics normally associated with humans. Of course God is a spirit being. Jesus had a hand – he was incarnated. Isaiah uses this anthropomorphic expression to indicate access, to make sure we understand the metaphors, because God is so amazing and holy and powerful, we would never understand him unless there was some kind of mechanism for doing so. It is as if God's hand is so big that the breadth of his hand marks off the heavens. 'Who has held the dust of the earth in a basket or weighed the mountains on the scales or the hills in a balance?' Nobody. Our God has got

the whole of the planet in his hands. What kind of god is that? No
other god is like that. He is the Lord of creation and he is the Lord of
destiny.

Who has instructed God?

Verse 13 – 'Who has understood the mind of the LORD or instructed
him as his counsellor?' Whom did the Lord consult? It is absolutely
fascinating because this refers, by implication, I am fairly sure, to an
incident in Babylonian mythology. Who did the Lord consult when
he made the earth? No one. The creator god of the Babylonians was
called Marduk. In the Babylonians epics and the myths of their creation stories, Marduk, the creator god, whom the Babylonians would
have seen as the equivalent of God, couldn't make the earth without
consultation and he actually consulted a higher god, called the all-wise
god, who was known as Ea – that is how he was translated into
English. Isaiah says to the people of God, by implication, Marduk the
creator god has to consult an even greater all-wise one in the
Babylonian mythology before he can create the world – he has to get
his advice. But our God – who has instructed him? No one. Who has
known his mind, who has given him advice – no one. He is the highest form of advice.

If you are in the professions, people probably seek your advice from
time to time. If you are doctor, they seek medical advice. If you are an
accountant, they seek financial advice. If you are a pastor, they seek
someone else's advice. And when the doctor doesn't know what is
wrong with you, he refers you to a specialist. The specialist doesn't
know what is wrong with you, so he sends you to London to see *the*
specialist. And *the* specialist knows the world's number one in New
York so he sends you to see him. And he says, 'It's a virus.'

Our God is without equal and he doesn't consult anybody else. He
is the greatest person who has ever lived and his mind is greater than
any other mind. He's the top of the chain, there is no one higher, and
he doesn't need to consult anybody else. 'Who was it that taught him
knowledge?' – verse 14. Nobody – verse 15. He's the Lord of the
nations – verse 15 – they are 'a drop in the bucket', one little dribble,

and they are like nothing. Isaiah says the nations of the world are like 'dust on the scales' – nothing. The Lord is the Lord of all the nations, he's Lord of creation, he's Lord of history and destiny, he's in charge – why is this important? Because if you have been in captivity for seventy years, firstly under the Babylonians and then under the Medeo-Persian empire, you will tend to believe that they were in charge of history and not God. But God is the God of history.

God is the Lord of all the nations and he is the Lord of all religious activity – verse 16. 'Lebanon is not sufficient for altar fires'; there aren't enough animals on the planet to provide enough burnt offerings to make him satisfied with religious observance. He is greater than all religious activity. Then verse 17 echoes verse 15 – the nations of the world are as nothing compared with him, less than nothing. He is in control. It really is him who is in charge. God is not only Lord of the nations (verses 18-20) he's the Lord of the idols.

You could hardly walk the streets of Babylon without seeing signs of this polytheistic culture and they were not just gods in theory; many of them would be occultic powers. There were also gods who were statues. Isaiah is saying they are nothing, they are things that are made: no one made our God, he's unmade, no one made him. 'Do you not know, (verse 21)? Have you not heard? Has it not been told you from the beginning?' Have you forgotten? 'Since the earth was founded,' it has been like this, he's the God of the Universe, not just the created order of the earth. 'He sits enthroned above the circle of the earth;' he's even outside, beyond all our experience of science and creation. To him, people are just like little dots ... 'grasshoppers. He stretches out the heavens like a canopy.' He's in charge of the whole universe. Haven't you heard? Where have you been? This is our God – and it is like a kind of whisper, a conspiratorial whisper, it is the opposite of our gossip circles. The gossip circles in churches are unbelievable. Isaiah stands the wickedness of gossip on its head and he says God is the Lord of the nations, he's the Lord of destiny, he's a God without equal, he's better than every single idol, haven't you heard?

He is without equal – the Christian God is the only God. Imagine hearing all this while you are tucked away in Babylon seeing if you dare set out on the journey home. God is a great God, there is no one like him, haven't you heard, they are preparing a place for us back in Jerusalem. It's a long way, it is going to be difficult, God is going to be with us, he's a great God, he's the only God. We know all this because we have the New Testament. I have read to the end of this book and we win!

Ours is a great big God, he is beyond compare. Don't you know? Haven't you heard? And then verse 23, absolute marvellous this, not only is he Lord of all these other things, God beyond compare and without equal, verse 23, 'He brings princes to naught and reduces the rulers of the world to nothing. No sooner are they planted (these rulers of the world) ... than he blows on them and they wither' and die. Who is in charge of our planet? Leaders have come and gone. Nebuchadnezzar the great – when he was around, you cowered. But he went. Darius the Mede – a significant Medeo-Persian leader; Alexander the Great, dominant for a very long time; the Roman Caesars, their vast reach over the ancient world; the horrors and brutality of Stalin, the megalomania of Adolf Hitler, they have all gone. Who rules the planet? The United Nations? The European Community? The Bush–Blair axis? I tell you this – the princes of this world will come to naught. Our God rules the world – leaders come and leaders go. God blows on them and they disappear.

Some months ago I found myself preaching in one of the largest churches in Romania, to a packed congregation. Almost every pastor that I met had been imprisoned for their faith under Ceascescu. I met with a group of pastors and they said 'For years we were encouraged because we believed that in the end, the leadership of the human race was not the determining factor in our destiny and that God was actually in charge. It wasn't the brutal bullying of Ceascescu that in the end would define our lives. Some of us would die under his regime, many of us would be oppressed, but in the end our God would determine the future of our nation.' That is faith in action.

We haven't known that in the UK, as yet, though we may know a persecution of sorts in the years to come. So God's in charge and again the repeat, the refrain from verse 18-25, '"To whom will you compare me? Or who is my equal?" says the Holy One.' Nobody, says Isaiah. I have been through it all and he is the Lord of everything. 'Lift your eyes and look to the heavens' − who created those stars? He called them out one by one. 'Because of his great power and mighty strength, not one of them is missing.' This is probably a military metaphor. God calls the stars out and has them on military parade and there isn't a single one of them missing, Isaiah says. In the ancient world, astral or occultic powers were worshipped in lots of places. People believed that their destiny was set by the stars. Isaiah says he is the Lord of the astral powers. These stars don't control your destiny. 'The One who flung stars in to space', to quote Graham Kendrick, he is the one who rules your destiny − the star Creator, not the star signs. He is greater than all the astral powers.

The God of hope

'Why do you say, O Jacob, and complain, O Israel? How can you possibly say that my way is hidden from the LORD?' 'This great God − how can anything be hidden from him? Do you think he didn't see you in your suffering in Babylon? How can you say,' says Isaiah, 'that you are not seen?' And it is quite interesting − this is another present continuous tense here − 'Why do you go on complaining, O Jacob and O Israel, that God can't see you, after all I have told you about his creating power, his Lordship of the universe? You're mad.'

'Don't you get it,' Isaiah says in verse 28, repeating what he has just said in verse 21, 'the LORD is the everlasting God.' The word Lord in the NIV there is capitalised and whenever that is the case, it refers to Yahweh, the I Am name for God, which we first come across in Exodus 3. He's the Yahweh, the I Am, the everliving one, Isaiah says. And he's the God of hope because he will always be there when you are in exile and when you are on your way back from exile. He created the ends of the earth and this is fabulous, this next bit, verse 28, halfway through, 'He will not grow tired or weary, and his understanding no-one can fathom. He gives strength to the weary and increases the power of the weak.'

These people were marching for four months, with babies being born on the way; the elderly, the crippled, the lame and the strong all together. In fact, Isaiah says, it is nothing to do with physical strength and he makes that point here, that physical energy is not what is in view. 'Even youths grow tired and weary, and young men stumble and fall.' Again the Hebrew is slightly complex here and it could be a military metaphor; even those fit enough to be recruited for the SAS. Or it could be an Olympic athletic metaphor: even those young men, the cream of the crop, ready to run in the Olympics. But whether they are the military most fit or the Olympic-level athletes, in the end even young people get tired. I find that such a relief. I like getting older because you can sound so superior when young people have so much energy. In the end, you'll get tired.

'Even youths grow tired and weary.' This march back to Jerusalem isn't going to be a canter, even for them, so divine help will be needed. It is 'those who hope in the LORD' – Yahweh – who 'will renew their strength'. Then what a marvellous metaphor to end with – 'They will soar on wings like eagles, they will (be able to) run, (never mind stumble along) and not grow weary, and they will (be able to) walk and not be faint.' 'I am going to get my people back out of exile and into the Promised Land. I'm going to give them supernatural strength and those who hope in me will be supernaturally supported and blessed and built up.' Our God is a God of rescue and comfort and help in time of exile, personally and corporately. God beyond compare and without equal, Lord of history and Lord of destiny, Lord of the astral powers, Lord of the universe, Lord of the nations, Lord of the princes, Lord of everything, and this same God is our God of hope. He will cause the young and the old and everything in between, though they may grow tired and weary, to mount up with wings like eagles – why? Because those that put their hope in God will know that kind of refuge and strength. May we today be encouraged by the greatness of our God, hope in him, soar on eagles' wings and have the hope of the living God in our hearts and minds and have the confidence to know as we go back home that our God is beyond compare and without equal.

The dawning of a new day (4)

Isaiah 43

Introduction

Yesterday in Isaiah 40, the scene shifted one hundred and fifty years to the end of the exilic period, and that passage moved us to focus on this great God. Now we continue that focus, this time on the new day, the new opportunity for the people of God. The scene is still the end of the exilic period; words delivered to encourage, to stimulate, to challenge, to bless this people as they are about to set off to return home to where they are meant to be. There is a lot of returning home in the Old Testament: the wilderness wanderings where Moses eventually gets the people to the Promised Land, back where they belong; and the Nebuchadnezzar exile, at the end of the 500s BC, which eventually sees them returning back home to the land. That's what's in view in this section.

Notice at the end of Isaiah 42, Israel is described as blind and deaf to what God wants to say. The metaphor is that they're enveloped in judgement: 42:25 reads 'So he poured out on them his burning anger, the violence of war. It enveloped them in flames, yet they did not understand; it consumed them, but they did not take it to heart.' We're going to see in a moment how the flames won't touch them because this is a new day. In the old day, the captivity, judgement was to be their lot. But this is a new day and Isaiah 43 begins with the phrase, 'But now' – it's God's great intervention.

I'm going to read these seven verses straight through to you in a moment, but as you listen, grasp hold of the 'But now' of God. 'It was judgement but now it's a new day, and I want you to focus on a new thing. It was recompense for sinfulness and rebellion but now it is a new day.' My prayer in this Bible reading is not just that we'll explore the Old Testament and reflect on the geography of the ancient world but that for many of us, God's 'But now' will become real. God will say, 'This is a new day and on this day I want to meet with you; to turn your life around.'

Fear not … Isaiah 43:1–7

'But now, this is what the LORD says …' Yahweh, the Ever-Living One '… he who created you, O Jacob, he who formed you, O Israel: "Fear not, for I have redeemed you; I have summoned you by name; you are mine. When you pass through the waters, I will be with you; and when you pass through the rivers, they will not sweep over you"' (Is. 43:1–2).

Do you sense the parallels with Isaiah 40? 'The mountains made low, the valleys filled up, when you go through rivers you won't be overwhelmed:' this is about the journey home.

> When you walk through the fire,
> you will not be burned;
> the flames will not set you ablaze.
> For I am the LORD, your God,
> the Holy One of Israel, your Saviour;
> I give Egypt for your ransom,
> Cush and Seba in your stead.
> Since you are precious and honoured in my sight,
> and because I love you,
> I will give men in exchange for you,
> and people in exchange for your life.
> Do not be afraid, for I am with you;

I will bring your children from the east
and gather you from the west.
I will say to the north, 'Give them up!'
and to the south, 'Do not hold them back.'
Bring my sons from afar
and my daughters from the ends of the earth –
everyone who is called by my name,
whom I created for my glory,
whom I formed and made (Is. 43:4-7).

Notice that the transformational elements which this passage will contain are hinted at in the very nomenclature of the early verse. 'This is what the LORD says' and this is the nomenclature to which I refer, 'he who created you, O Jacob, he who formed you, O Israel'. That's an absolutely fascinating prophetic device Isaiah uses to get us into the material. Between chapters 40 and 49 this couplet, 'O Jacob, O Israel' occurs thirteen times. It's a recurring motif of Isaiah's understanding of the way God works, in transitional mode. Why is this important?

Change is possible

In the Bible, names are significant and this group have gone from being a nation named after Jacob to being a nation named after Israel. You might say, 'They're the same person.' I agree but what does the name 'Jacob' mean? It means 'cheat' or 'supplant'. Jacob was a great con artist. He tricked his semi-blind father. He even tricked his exhausted brother Esau. So Jacob means 'cheat' but Israel is a much more honoured name for the nation as a whole. Isaiah's implication is that they came from a cheat who was restored by a touch from God. That story is some kind of theophany, God appearing in the Old Testament. Jacob's hip is put out of joint and he limps for ever after that but he's more whole spiritually than he's ever been before, after that incident. So he goes from being Jacob to being Israel, touched and transformed by God.

The names are significant, they mean things. We've already commented on Maher-halal-hash-baz. For example, my name is 'Stephen' which means 'crown' and my middle name is 'John' which means 'prince' or 'beloved' so my name means 'the beloved crown prince.' No one thinks about that in our culture, but in Old Testament culture they did. Isaiah is sending us the signal that the cheat need not always remain the cheater: transformation to Israel is possible. The name of Jacob is a synonym for the whole nation rather than just an individual and he says 'You saw that transformation, you know it took place, God met with this person, he was no longer this, he became that. You are now in exile struggling, despairing, you are this, but in just the same way you can become that – transition is possible, change can happen.'

Isn't it a problem for many of us, that we frankly don't believe we can change? We don't believe it at a personal level. 'I've always had a bad temper, I'm always going to have a bad temper.' I remember a man speaking to me after a meeting once, incredibly rudely, and he said, 'I'm blunt and I don't apologise for that.' Someone should have said to him, 'You don't have to apologise for being blunt, you need to apologise for being rude!' Sometimes we say, 'It's just who I am,' and some may say that about church: 'Our church has always been like this, it'll never be any different.' Was Jacob forever condemned to be Jacob? No. Transformation is possible. Were the children forever condemned to be under Babylonian oppression? No. Deliverance is possible.

The ownership of the people of God

Why is this? Because the ownership of the people of God is a threefold ownership in the Old Testament and it's a threefold ownership today. It's defined in these verses. Notice this: 'But now, this is what the LORD says – he who created you, O Jacob, he who formed you, O Israel' (verse 1). That's a literary device often used in the psalms; repetition for emphasis. For example, Psalm 34 begins 'I will bless the LORD at all times.' The next phrase is 'His praise shall continually be in my mouth.' What's the difference in meaning between those two phrases? Next to nothing; they're basically repetitive phrases for emphasis. The difference between creation and formation in this context is minimal; it's merely a repetition for emphasis.

'I created you so don't be afraid; I have redeemed you, and I have called you or summoned you by name' and then the little three word summary 'so you're mine' (verse 2). 'That's why you're going to be delivered; because you're mine, I created you, I redeemed you, and I have called you by name. That's why you're going to be set free from your captivity. I haven't forgotten you. I made you a nation in the first place, through Abraham, through Isaac, through Jacob; your existence as a Jewish people is no cosmic accident. I created you. I redeemed you – I've paid the price for you again and again and again. I've called you my people, my name I have placed upon you, and in those three ways you are mine. And I have responsibility for you. I've a covenant relationship with you', says God. 'You're mine. I'm not just going to leave you there to languish forever in exilic pain.'

What's true for the nation is true for individuals. They were created by God, they have been redeemed and they have been called by name. There's a lovely little story from one of the northern states in America, about a little boy, whose father was a carpenter. The boy made himself a boat, which he crafted and painted with care. He sailed the boat down the local creek, which became a river. To his incredible dismay, it rushed away across some rapids. He was unable to get it and months of hard work disappeared down into the rushing river. Dispirited and tearful, he went home and condolences were expressed by his parents. Some months later, in the pawn shop right in the centre of town, to his complete amazement, he saw his boat in the window. He went in and he said to the man 'That's my boat!' and the man said 'It's not your boat. Someone found it and I bought it from them and it's for sale.' So the little boy saved his money over weeks and eventually went back and bought the boat again from the man and this time, touching up the paint, wrote his name and address on the boat. This boat belonged to the boy three times. He made it, he bought it back and he called it by his name.

That's exactly what God has done for us. He made us, he's redeemed us and he's called us by name. If you know Jesus Christ as your Saviour and Lord, I promise you, you were made by him, in your mother's womb. Of course, the normal biological processes were in action but the creative Genius of the universe was involved in your creation. You've been redeemed if you're a Christian; not by a vague ransom but by the specific redemptive act of Christ on the cross, who took all of God's wrath and anger into himself. All the separation and wickedness of humanity, the flaming sword at the Garden of Eden, which was a symbol of separation, was plunged into the heart of Christ and extinguished there on our behalf. He died in our place, we are redeemed as the people of God, and we're called 'Christian', followers of Christ. We are created by God, we are redeemed by God, and we are called by God; and he says these three words of each of us who know him: 'You are mine.'

That's great, isn't it? We belong to God. He says 'mine' about us; no wonder our destiny isn't some fluke or accident; no wonder we needn't fear about the future. Whatever happens to us, we're his! We belong to him – and Isaiah is trying to say to this beleaguered people, 'You were made, redeemed and named by the living God. Never forget who you are!'

There was a French foot soldier brought to Napoleon. He was on trial for desertion and Napoleon said, 'What did you do?' He said, 'I ran away.' Napoleon looked at him and said, 'What's your name?' The soldier said 'Napoleon.' Napoleon said to him, 'Change your name or change your behaviour.' We are named Christians, we're called to live in that particular way – living up to the name of the people of God. They weren't just a ragtag and bobtail band in Babylon. They were still God's people there in exile.

Don't be afraid

Notice the motif of the 'Fear nots'. Halfway through verse 1, 'Fear not, for I have redeemed you' and then again in verse 5, 'Do not be afraid.' It's one of the things Jesus really enjoyed saying to his disciples. 'Don't be afraid. You needn't fear because I made you, I paid the price for you, and I have called you by name. And so when you pass through the waters I'm going to be with you. They won't sweep over you, and the fire won't burn you.' God invited them to think back in their history to his wonderful, miraculous deliverance. 'Do you remember when you crossed the Red Sea, you were not consumed although the Egyptian army were. What a miracle! You remember when you crossed the Jordan, you were able to get across safely.' It's possible that the fires referred to here are a hint in connection with Daniel about the fiery furnace; we don't know for sure. 'The fire won't consume you, mighty rivers won't wash you away, you will be able to get back home because I am going to be with you.' 'For I am the LORD, your God, the Holy One of Israel, your Saviour' (verse 3).

Skip down to verse 11: 'I, even I, am the LORD, and apart from me there is no saviour.' Notice again the challenge to the polytheistic Babylonian context. 'I made you, redeemed you and named you, don't be afraid because as you journey back home, all this way, you won't be obliterated by the geographical and military challenges you face on the way. I will be with you, I am the LORD your God the Holy One and I am the only Saviour. And all these other gods won't help you and they can't resist me, just in case you think they are big enough to resist me.'

That's the problem for many of us: we live in a world in which God's power doesn't seem very evident and so we start to lose confidence that God is capable of coming up with the goods, and of delivering what he says he'll deliver. But twice in this chapter he makes it clear that he is the only Saviour, only he can set them free. Remember we said yesterday, the thing that's going to get us into trouble in the next twenty years in the UK is not saying that Jesus is God but saying that Jesus is the only God. The uniqueness of this Saviour … there is no other Saviour.

'For I am the LORD your God, I'm the only saviour; no one else can get you out of Babylon. And I'm going to make the empire around you' – that will become the Medeo-Persian empire, following on from the Chaldeans. They'll attack other nations and Egypt will be given for a ransom. Cush is probably another name for the Upper Nile region and Seba, verse 3, is probably a reference to somewhere in the Sudan. It's quite difficult to be absolutely sure. 'I will give people in exchange for you' (verse 4) is the definition of ransom. 'I'll buy you back, so do not be afraid.'

Come home

Then comes the great call to the people of God to stream back to the holy city. Look at these wonderful verses: 'I will bring your children from the east' (verse 6), which is where Babylon was, 'and from the west' actually there wasn't much west apart from the Mediterranean and a little bit of where the Philistines were. 'From the north' means Lebanon and Syria, 'from the south', which is back to Egypt and the Sudan and maybe the southern tip of Jordan. 'Don't hold them back. Bring my sons and daughters, gather them'. Then we have verse 7's repetition, 'everyone who is called by my name, created and formed by me', which is a repetition of the first section in verse 1 and 2.

'Come back home!' Isaiah encourages them: they'll be coming from everywhere, not just exile in Babylon. Wherever God's people have been, they're going to gather together. There are hints here also of a further prophetic horizon, one following the first coming of Jesus, when God's people will gather in some form or other, ready for his glorious, magnificent eventual return. 'Come home!' says Isaiah. 'From all over the four points of the compass, come back to the holy city.' And he imagines them trickling and then streaming back to the place called home. From the east and from the west and the north and the south they're returning: 'Come home!' says Isaiah. 'Come back. Have the confidence to return.'

This is prodigal stuff, like the prodigal son in the New Testament. 'Come home, you've been in the pigsty long enough, you've been in exile long enough, come home.' I love the story of the prodigal son. I'm sure Isaiah didn't know it. But the people of God were prodigal, no question. They were in the pigsty for sure, they hated where they were. But God brought them home. Finished, washed up, miles from home, here they are the children of God. Broken, defeated: here's the call from all the points of the globe and the four points of the compass, to return back to the living God: 'Come home.'

Verse 8 is the antithesis of 42:18; 'Lead out those who have eyes but are blind, who have ears but are deaf ...' What has he said in 42:18? 'Hear, you deaf; look, you blind, and see!' But they didn't, so the deaf didn't hear and the blind didn't see. Now the deaf do hear and the blind do see; this is a new day.

For time's sake, I'll be quite selective in these particular verses. Verse 13, 'Yes, and from ancient days, I am he. No one can deliver out of my hand. When I act, who can reverse it?' I love that phrase. When God acts, who can reverse it? God says, 'I'm calling you back home! I'm defeating every god and every obstacle that stands in the way of that return. When I act, who can reverse it?' What human can say that? What a great God we have.

Verse 14 following talks about God's mercy, even in the face of Israel's unfaithfulness to him. Daniel and the three friends were faithful but many of the Jews who were taken into exile did not manage such faithfulness. Verse 15: 'I am the LORD, your Holy One, Israel's Creator, your King.' And then verse 16 again calls them to remember the Red Sea and Jordan experiences. Look at this: 'he who made a way through the sea, a path through the mighty waters, who drew out the chariots and horses, the army and reinforcements together, and they lay there, never to rise again'. The Egyptian army was obliterated.

Forget the past … Isaiah 43:18,19

Verses 18 and 19 are pivotal, not just to chapter 43 but to this entire section from 40 to 55, because they come as such a shock. Isaiah has been saying again and again and again to the people, 'Don't you get it? Haven't you heard? God does love you, he made you, he redeemed you, he's named you, and think back – did he not get you across the Red Sea? Yes! Did he not get you across the Jordan? Yes! Has he not been faithful to you? Yes! Remember all that.' Then suddenly he says something that seems starkly contradictory, verse 18: 'Forget the former things'. Wait a minute! Haven't you just been telling us to remember the former things? 'Forget the former things; do not dwell on the past. See, I am doing a new thing! Now it springs up; do you not perceive it? I am making a way in the desert' and so on.

The Hebrew here is not gentle, it's strong. 'Forget the past!' It's that sort of strength here. 'Forget the former things!' How do we square that with 'remember the past'? What Isaiah is trying to do, remembering back to his great experience in the temple, is trying to help the people of God with a lesson we'd do well to learn. He is trying to deliver them from a religion of nostalgia to a religion of expectation. It's crippled churches and Christians for years. He wants them to remember the past in the sense that there is continuity between the past and the present and the future. God's character doesn't change, but he wants them also to remember that in the precise way God acts, there is discontinuity as well as continuity. He does new things in each generation because new things need to be done, depending on the context.

The way worship needed to happen in Egypt when they were a slave people was one thing, but the way worship happened in forty years of wilderness wandering, with a tent called a tabernacle, was another completely different thing. Under David and Solomon and so on, worship with a temple happened in a completely different way. Then when they were whisked away to exile for seventy years, worship couldn't possibly happen in the same way because there wasn't the temple there. At each phase of the Israelite history, God didn't change but his operational activity did, to meet the new circumstances. The trouble was, the children of Israel were forever getting nostalgic: not about God's character, which would have been perfectly appropriate, but nostalgic about his specific activity. Do you know what they did when they were in the wilderness with Moses? They were always complaining. He'd got them out of slavery, after ten plagues; it was hell in Goshen, they were beaten bloody by the Egyptian rulers, and after a few years in the wilderness, what are they saying? 'It was so lovely back in Egypt; we had such a great time. Can't we go back?' How quickly people forget. You see, they were nostalgic. And as you get older, the great danger is to have a religion of nostalgia. 'Wasn't it great when we knew all the hymns? If God had meant us to have PowerPoint words, he would never have invented the overhead projector!' Churches and individuals can get enveloped in nostalgia. It was all so easy then. Yesterday was great but today, oh my goodness!

We have got to wake up to the fact that our God never changes. Remember his activity on the Red Sea, his activity in the Jordan, his activity subduing the Canaan people, his activity in restoring the Promised Land, his activity again and again through all the prophets; remember that: we don't need a religion of nostalgia but a religion of expectation. God wants to do a new thing, a fresh thing. The church is crushed in our nation, at times, by those who live with nostalgia. Those of us who live with that kind of nostalgia are cramping God's style, limiting his ability to do fresh things. We've got to understand the difference between divine principles which never change, which we must keep remembering, and cultural expressions. They're so, so different. Thirty or forty years ago as I was growing up in evangelicalism, there was an extremely clear view about the use of alcohol. Abstinence was the rule. It never occurred to me to question that. Here we are thirty years later: many, many evangelicals have a completely different attitude to alcohol. I promise you, you cannot prove abstinence as the biblical position on alcohol from Scripture. But when I grew up, I assure you people said you could. We've got to get a life about issues which are cultural and learn the difference. This is why I'm so passionate about letting the Bible speak for itself. How else will you know what is cultural and what isn't?

I've been married for twenty-four years. My wife's an American. When we first came to this country, things were very different. And my wife arrived from the southern States with pierced ears. Somehow I had to convince people that a woman with pierced ears could go to heaven! I remember the battles. I spoke at a meeting, and Jan sang a solo, and then I preached. Afterwards, we had the most vitriolic letter. 'How could you allow your wife to wear those dangly earrings in God's house?' I didn't like to say I couldn't stop her. God does not care that much for these issues. I promise you, he does not care! And we as evangelicals have got to get a life! Because if we don't, we'll spend all our time arguing about complete nonsense and the world around us will go to hell while we argue about trivia.

Forget the former things, if they are merely cultural; remember them, if they are of divine and inspired origin. Only remember them if that's the case. 'See, I am doing a new thing.' Thank God for that, the religion not of nostalgia but of expectation. Can God set you and me free from habits of a lifetime? Can he do something in our nation, in our day, that's different? Could he set the people free from Babylon? They all thought the answer to that would be 'No'. We'll be here forever, many of them thought; only the faithful few believed it was possible for God to lead them back across the wilderness and the desert.

Verse 19: 'I am making a way in the desert' hints again of John the Baptist. I am making it possible for 'the people I have formed for myself that they may proclaim my praise' (verse 21). Look at verse 25: 'I, even I, am he who blots out your transgressions for my own sake, and remembers your sins no more.' 'I can do it, I am capable of doing it; I will do it!'

When people make promises to us, we base it on their ability to deliver. When God promises, only he can deliver. 'Jacob, you've become Israel; remember that personal transformation. Do you think I can get you out of Babylon? Yes I can. And I am calling you home,' says Isaiah. 'Come home from the north, the south, and the east and the west, come back to where you are meant to be, in Jerusalem. Because I've made you, I've redeemed you, I've called you; don't be afraid.'

It's possible for you to do that, like the prodigal, to come back today to God; come and meet him, come and know him. Let the deep, deep love of Jesus wash over you and overwhelm you in his forgiveness. He's the one who can blot out every sin. He's the one who can forgive you. He's the one, the only Saviour, and now because we have the revelation of the New Testament, we know that the only Saviour is personified not simply in the Yahweh God but in the Christ child Jesus. Only Jesus can save us. It's a new day but now God's going to do a new thing, now we can be forgiven, now we can move on, now we can take a new start and we can get out of Babylon and head off to Jerusalem, that God's name may be glorified and blessed among us.

The great invitation (5)

Isaiah 55

Introduction

The central verse of this chapter, Isaiah 55, is as relevant right now in 2005 as it was whenever Isaiah first uttered it in the 740s BC. Isaiah 55 is the culmination of the prophetic words to encourage the people as they begin to leave Babylonian exile. Looking ahead down the vistas of the years, Isaiah, under the inspiration of the Holy Spirit, sees this bedraggled, oppressed people needing all the encouragement they can get to return to the Lord. To return to him emotionally, to return to him physically, making this journey from Babylon in the east back to Jerusalem.

The suffering Servant

The exact context of Isaiah 55 is the songs of the suffering servant. Flick back to Isaiah 53 and you'll see an extremely well-known passage which has both Christmas and Easter overtones. Verses 4-6; 'Surely he took up our infirmities and carried our sorrows, yet we considered him stricken by God, smitten by him and afflicted. But he was pierced for our transgressions, he was crushed for our iniquities; the punishment that brought us peace was upon him and by his wounds we are all healed. We all, like sheep, have gone astray' and so on. Isaiah postulates this suffering Servant: sometimes identified with the people of God, or Isaiah himself, or with other people who served the people of God but ultimately identified with a coming Messiah who will transform not just the fortunes of the people of God, the Jews, but those of the entire planet.

The great context of Isaiah 55 is the suffering Servant who gives himself for the benefit of the people.

> Come, all you who are thirsty,
> come to the waters;
> and you who have no money,
> come, buy and eat!
> Come, buy wine and milk
> without money and without cost.
> Why spend money on what is not bread,
> and your labour on what does not satisfy?
> Listen, listen to me, and eat what is good,
> and your soul will delight in the richest of fare.
> Give ear and come to me;
> hear me, that your soul may live.
> I will make an everlasting covenant with you,
> my faithful love promised to David.
> See, I have made him a witness to the peoples,
> a leader and commander of the peoples.
> Surely you will summon nations you know not,
> and nations that do not know you will hasten to you,
> because of the LORD your God,
> the Holy One of Israel,
> for he has endowed you with splendour.
> Seek the LORD while he may be found;
> call on him while he is near.
> Let the wicked forsake his way
> and the evil man his thoughts.
> Let him turn to the LORD, and he will have mercy on him,
> and to our God, for he will freely pardon (Is. 55:1-6).

This chapter has two rising crescendo points. The first crescendo ends at the end of verse 7. Then verses 8 and 9 transition us into the mind of God himself and the incredible promises of what this everlasting sign will be, the guarantee that the future of the children of God may have its ups and downs but its spirituality (because it's all wrapped up in the suffering Servant) will be guaranteed and permanent.

Pay attention

There is one or two slightly technical things to start with about this chapter. Isaiah is noted for little expressions which are almost impossible to translate. Turn over in your Bible to Isaiah 64, verse 1. What word begins Isaiah 64? The word 'Oh'. That's quite an odd little interjection. In some of our hymns we've got so used to saying it that we've forgotten that in our culture it doesn't mean anything. Take the carol, 'O come all ye faithful'. What does 'O' mean? 'Come all ye faithful,' you could say. But in a slightly different usage of English from centuries ago, the 'O' was some kind of call. At the beginning of Isaiah 55, it's a call to pay attention. Although the NIV is a masterful translation, I think it's wrong at this point. I wonder if anybody has with them the King James Version, the 1611 version of Scripture? What is the first word of Isaiah 55 in your translation? 'Ho'! What does that mean? Is it something to do with Plymouth? No. It actually translates a Hebrew word which is hardly a word at all, it's transliteration into English is h-o-i and maybe 'Ho' is the nearest thing to it. The NIV translates it 'Come' and it misses out the fact that Isaiah is trying to get our attention. 'Ho everyone who thirsts.' I'm tempted to say the best translation would be 'Oi!' except that's far too crude and because 'Oi' is not quite right. 'Oi' is a rude interjection. This is not a Ho of aggression, it's almost a sigh: it's got sadness about it. It's almost an exhalation of breath, saying 'Have I yet got your attention?'

'Pay attention,' Isaiah says using this little breathing word, 'listen to this.' It's not going to be loud and magnificent and splendid and transcendent, as much of Isaiah is: it's going to be understated, quite quiet. But it's going to be profound, significant and pastorally potent. So ignore the first 'Come' in the NIV and simply breathe deeply, perhaps with a touch of sadness, that the people of God have so far failed to do this. 'All you who are thirsty'; it's imperative, 'Come to the water.' 'Come' 'buy' and 'eat' are all plural but the first statement is singular. It's as if to say, 'This invitation is to all of you together but you must come individually.' The great danger of all exposition of the word, all reading of Scripture, is that at times we assume the message is for somebody else, because the word 'you' in English can be both singular and plural. We evade the impact of the word by imagining that the preacher is addressing other people.

Isaiah must have had that problem. There were Jews in Babylon who'd made quite a good living for themselves. They excelled in tradesmen's skills and they may have been reluctant to return home. Which would you choose: a nice little earner you've got in a backstreet in Babylon selling things, or back to the wrecked damage of a Jerusalem where the infrastructure is hardly conducive to commerce and economy, the political situation is ripe for revolution, the walls are broken down, the temple remains are shattered, even the delivery of clean water seems to have been compromised? Which would you choose? Isaiah is having to lever them out of their comfort zones. It would be easy for them to think, 'This is just for those people who have had a wretched time here.' No, it is singularly appropriate. The finger points at me but the invitation is universal. 'Come, all of you.'

Free but not cheap

Isaiah seems to have in mind the Middle Eastern water-seller. People sold water in huge quantities in the ancient world, because the access to clean water was life itself. So a water-seller would often be wandering around market places, doling out water which had been gathered from a spring, sometimes carried on a cart pulled by a donkey. The water crier comes into the street selling water. 'Come,' says Isaiah, 'buy and eat. All you who are thirsty, come to the waters and you who have no money' ... 'you who have not made it as tradesmen in Babylon; the outcast, the refugee, the asylum seeker, the sad, the lonely, the person on the edge of society, on the periphery, marginalised by its wealth:

come even though you've got nothing and the Servant will give you water.'

Have you noticed the apparent contradiction? 'You who have no money, come buy and eat'? How can they buy it if they don't have any money? This is not some kind of spiritual soup kitchen. This is not Isaiah saying, 'There's this great big hand-out.' This food is free but it is not cheap. It has a purchase price and the implication of this whole passage is that a price has been paid. God has paid the price.

Have you noticed how if you pay nothing for something, you don't value it? If someone gives you something free, you wonder what's wrong with it and you don't treat it with respect. But if you pay a lot of money for something, you treat it with a great deal more respect. Isaiah is keen to point out to these people that just because the gift is free, they mustn't abuse that generosity of God, believing it came without a cost. There's a wonderful hint in almost all of Isaiah, particularly in this passage, of a Saviour who paid the price. Is salvation free? Answer of course. You can't earn it, you can't buy it, you can't be clever enough to get it.

It's not salvation through works. It's salvation by him paying the price on our behalf. The great ransom that will be paid is not without cost to somebody. The suffering Servant has to suffer. The production of the ransom is real but to these starving, alienated, sad recipients, it's free. It costs nothing to come to this same God that Isaiah called his people to.

What satisfies?

Why spend money on what is not bread? Why are you focused on trivia, on earning this good living in Babylon? It won't satisfy you. It's food that doesn't satisfy. There's a little diet thing going on here because he then says, 'Eat food that does satisfy.' Have you noticed that some foods satisfy and some foods don't? 'Why do you work for food that does not satisfy? All this money you've got in Babylon, all this stuff you've acquired, it sounds great and makes your life feel good, but it will not satisfy you.'

From time to time, once a year or so, I go on a diet. It's not I'm massively overweight, but roughly once a year my wife gently pats my tummy and says 'When is it due?' I take that subtle hint to mean I ought to do something about my dietary activity. I eat out all the time, I have meetings over breakfast, lunch and dinner. The trouble with meetings over food is that while you're talking, you're just eating … When I have those meetings, I get to the end of the meal and I've no idea what I've had. So I go on this salad regime and twenty minutes after I've eaten it, I feel hungry again. I need to eat something. The prophet says, 'Why are you obsessed with getting all this food and drink that doesn't satisfy, when I am offering you the living water that does satisfy?' Doesn't that remind you of Jesus, constantly telling the people they would never be satisfied?

Brothers and sisters, I want to say the same thing to you. You will never earn enough, you will never get a high enough status, you will never get enough fame, nothing will ever satisfy you, apart from knowing Jesus. The Bible is replete with this kind of teaching. 'Come, drink the living water,' says Isaiah. 'You're never going to be satisfied otherwise. And you'll delight in the richest of fare.' The spiritual banquet is coming. There's so much in the Bible about feasting. We're all headed for a great feast. The richest of fare is simply an anticipation of an eschatological event in which the food will be sumptuous beyond our wildest dreams. The marriage supper of the Lamb is coming. Feast now on him and enjoy the richest of fare and anticipate that day when, with every saint from every nation, we will dine at the heavenly table, feasting for ever with him. What a glorious picture that is.

'Don't get absorbed in materialistic endeavour,' says Isaiah. 'Drink in that which is good for you.' Notice the word 'Come' continues here: 'Come to me,' 'Come to me,' 'Come to me' – 'Come back to God.' 'Give ear to me' – 'I'm going to make this everlasting covenant with you, I promised something to David, and I'm going to keep my promise to him.'

The God of the nations

Verse 5 is a stunning revelation: 'Surely you will summon nations you know not, and nations you do not know will hasten to you, because of the LORD your God, the Holy One of Israel, for he has endowed you with splendour.' Isaiah has a very advanced missiology. He actually understands that the Holy One of Israel is not only for the people of God, but there will be a point when the nations of the world will be coming to Yahweh, the one true God, the Holy One of Israel. In his prophetic imagination he sees the day when the Holy One of Israel will be established as the Holy One of the whole earth. The prophets continue to talk about this, that they will be drawn from all over the world, and the glory of the Lord will cover the earth as the waters cover the sea. There's a lot of this in the prophetic literature. It's beyond the people we know about. It's those sheep yet in other folds, other nations summoned to God. It's not just for our language group or nationality: God is interested in the nations of the world, drawing them to himself with love, grace and passion.

Take a step

This section climaxes in what must be the best-known verses of this section in Isaiah: 'Seek the LORD while he may be found; call on him while he is near.' There's a positive and a negative here. I'd like to draw your attention to both of them. 'Seek the LORD and call on him'. The Hebrew word for 'seeking' doesn't have the idea behind it of looking for something that's lost. It's not that God's lost and they don't know where to find him. It is to do with a tread, as in a step, and it literally means 'take steps towards God'. It's quite an evocative metaphor because they've got to take steps out of Babylon to get back to Jerusalem. Isaiah says 'Seek God': he's talking spiritually now, not just about the journey. 'Take a step towards God.' It's a step from the security of the city into the wilderness, into insecurity, but when you step towards God, you'll find him. You can have the safety of Babylon or you can step out and seek the Lord, is the implication.

Some of us are fearful. God's saying 'Seek the LORD while he may be found, call on him while he is near.' Seek him, call him, take a step out. God's calling some of us to take a step towards him, not a step away from him. Some of us are stepping out of our comfort zones into something frightening, a new role, a difficult situation, we're not sure we want to seek the Lord particularly. Our Christian life's fine as it is and the idea of stepping towards him is a little frightening.

I remember some years ago, Jan and I were in Northern Ireland. Just down the Antrim coast from Giant's Causeway there's a little island which you get to over a rope bridge. We went with our son, Sam, who was ten. We're standing on the edge of this rope bridge and Sam was absolutely terrified. The bridge is blowing in the wind, it's very narrow, with little slats across, and it's a huge drop down to the ocean below. He wouldn't step onto it. Jan had gone charging ahead because Jan is the brave one in our family. She's the one whose been hang-gliding, she'd do bungee jumping, whereas I'm a tiddly-winks man, myself. Sam's nervous and he won't go, he won't step out, and he's too big to carry. But eventually we got all the way to the other side and he was so thrilled. Then he turned round and realised he was going to have to go back. But that journey into the unknown for him began with the tread, the first step into the unknown, keeping his eyes on his mum at the other end. What Isaiah's saying here is, 'God's not lost.' It's not that the children of Israel didn't know where God was, they'd just got to take a step towards him. Tread out towards him … seek the Lord.

Call on him

The other metaphor is, 'Call on him', ask for him to respond to you. The metaphor is of someone interrupting someone who's busy. It's as if God is just longing for a tap on the shoulder. He's more than ready to turn, he's waiting for our call, he wants us to come to him, he's desperate for a relationship with us, so will we tread out towards him? Will we call out to him and get his attention? And when we do call to him and seek him, then he will be found. This is the day to seek the Lord, to tread out towards him, to call on his name.

That's the positive. God's longing for us to seek him and to call him but here's the negative, and I say it with sadness and reluctance. It's quite difficult to explain because it's about the character of God and his sovereign purposes, which I am not privy to. But there's a hint in this verse which is serious. 'Seek the LORD' and then the caveat –

'while he may be found; call on him while he is near.' The clear implication of Isaiah's confrontation with the people of God is this: seek him while he's near, call on him while he can be found, because there may come a time when he isn't near and can't be found. I don't quite understand that; that's quite a frightening thought. Imagine that thought addressed to us. Imagine God's been speaking to us for years about a particular habit, imagine he's been desperate for us to seek him and call him and we imagine any time we're ready, we can seek God and he will be found. There is a hint here and I don't say more than that because only God knows his timing. But could it be that there will be a time when he's not able to be found? Maybe our hearts will be too hard for us to turn to him. That's a very serious suggestion in this passage. What if there comes a point when we have rejected him for so long that he is not capable of being found by us; not because he is resistant, but because we have robbed ourselves of that ability by resisting him for so long?

Guard your heart

What is the call? 'Let the wicked forsake his way and the evil man his thoughts. Let him turn to the LORD, and he will have mercy on him, and to our God, for he will freely pardon'... We're back to 'free' again; free wine, free water, free pardon. That's the call to us: 'Forsake your wicked ways and your wicked thoughts.' Have you noticed the link between those two things? Both in Isaiah's teaching and in the Scripture as a whole, thoughts and activities are very closely linked together. We think a thought first and our activity follows. It is true, in the grossest of sins, that the sin almost always starts weeks, months or years before in our thought life. People don't just wake up one morning and decide to commit adultery. What usually has happened is over weeks and months, our thought life has got out of control and in the end inappropriate thinking has resulted in inappropriate action. That's why we should guard our hearts, the Bible says, guard our thought processes.

Let the wicked forsake his thoughts because once you've thought this, you're on a journey. Jesus said if you look at a woman with adultery in your heart, it's like committing adultery with her. Now clearly, if you've got to do one of those two, it's much better to only think about it. But Jesus was on to something, psychologically, pastorally, spiritually and theologically. The wicked often start off by thinking the wrong things and that leads to the wrong kind of activity. Isaiah challenges all of us is to forsake our wicked thoughts in order that we will go on forsaking wicked actions. When we do that and turn to God and seek him, he abundantly, freely, pardons; it doesn't cost anything. It's already cost God the death of his Son but it won't cost us a penny. We can receive that freedom beautifully, wonderfully and totally free of charge.

A free pardon

Some people find it very difficult to forgive themselves. They've done something wrong and they feel they ought to pay for it; they can't believe that God's mercy is free. They feel they have to suffer or atone for it or earn the right to be forgiven. It is terribly, terribly painful sometimes, to be forgiven. I remember, as a little boy, being up in my bedroom. A friend of mine had come home from school and we were playing in my bedroom and we'd got those old school satchels filled with books and we were throwing them at each other. He threw the satchel at me and I caught it and went back through my bedroom window, which was closed at the time. The glass shattered onto the path below and I caught myself in the frame. My first thought was, my father will be home in half an hour. When he came home, I rushed out to meet him, because I thought it would be better to confront the enemy head on.

I've never forgotten my father's response and I've never forgiven him for it. He said to me, 'Steve, that's fine. These things happen.' How could he? I was waiting for him to be cross with me. It would have been much easier for him to shout at me, send me to my room, ban my pocket money for three weeks … I'd have felt much better about that! That was what I deserved. But when he forgave me, I felt really awful, which of course was what he had in mind.

Some of us can't forgive ourselves. That's our problem. We doubt God's grace. We don't call it that; we say 'Oh I've been too terrible. No,

I can't …' but in the end we doubt God's grace. The pardon Isaiah offered the people of God, as individuals and corporately, is a totally free pardon.

We often quote the next verse, verse 8, totally out of context, whenever we want to say that God's bigger than us: '"For my thoughts are not your thoughts, neither are your ways my ways," declares the LORD. "As the heavens are higher than the earth, so are my ways higher than your ways, and my thoughts than your thoughts."' Notice the context, at the end of verse 7. 'Let him turn … to our God for he will freely pardon.' Freely pardon? Who does that? Using Isaiah as his voice, God says, 'My ways are not your ways.' You would not freely pardon! 'I want what I'm due. You've done this. I want you to pay me back.' Free pardon is not part of the human equation. But, says God, 'My ways are not your ways. I'm God, you aren't. And so I abundantly and freely pardon you.'

How reliable are you?

Verse 11 is another of those evangelical hot verses, 'so is my word that goes out from my mouth: it will not return to me empty but will accomplish what I desire and achieve the purpose for which I sent it.' How will God give me a free pardon? How do I know when I seek him, he'll respond and when I call on him, he will reply? Well, you can trust God's word because as he speaks it, he accomplishes his purpose. The Hebrew thought form here is that the spoken word and the action which follows it are so close together as to be impossible to separate. One of the best illustrations is in Genesis, in the creation story, where God says 'Let there be light' and what is the very next sentence? 'And there was light.' God's word accomplishes exactly what he says. God is so powerful that his word and his activity are as one. Now that's totally unhuman. How many of us say a word and it's never fulfilled at all? I've lost count of the number of people I ring up and they say 'Steve, I don't know the answer to that but I will call you back on Friday.' Weeks go by!

In the word of God when he speaks, the word and the activity which follows it are so close as to be utterly joined, absolutely reliable. When God speaks, it will accomplish the purpose for which he sends it out. It's not in doubt, it's not a wishful thinking exercise, it's not a vain hope. It will accomplish it; when God says 'I'll bring my people back from the land of Babylon' he will do it. 'Let there be light' – there was light. When God says he'll freely pardon, he'll freely pardon. He doesn't lie. He's not like human beings. He doesn't do that. God's word accomplishes that which it is designed to accomplish.

Here, finally, is the great promise. Because of the suffering Servant, and all God will accomplish through the life, death and resurrection of Jesus (that's not explicitly stated of course in this chapter but by implication) what's going to happen is, you will be led out in joy and led forth in peace ... You know the song? There will be a great celebration. 'Instead of thorns, there'll be a pine tree' – what does this mean? And 'instead of briers' – actually probably the literal translation in the Hebrew of brier is stinging nettle – 'instead of stinging nettles, the myrtle will grow'. So what's good about pine trees and myrtles? I had to do a lot of research about pine trees and nettles and this is what I found out. Pine trees are nicer than nettles. It's true. It's what every commentator says about this.

Actually there's one rather more subtle point and with this I close. What's the significance about the pine and the myrtle tree? They are evergreens. They are forever something good and green and at their best; they're not weeds or shrubs or nettles. They are something substantial and something year-round. 'This is going to be the sign,' says Isaiah, 'that you're going to have year-round knowledge of who this God is and your life, which may have been nettly, is about to look far more like a myrtle tree or a pine.' Some things are destroyed by the onset of winter but an evergreen isn't. 'I am going to give you a sign'. The first sign will be the return from exile to Jerusalem, and the signs which follow, the suffering Servant, is the sign of Jesus Christ coming into the world. And because Isaiah was right and because Jesus came, people across the globe may yet seek him, may yet call on him, and may yet live for ever in his glorious kingdom.

The Lecture

Week One – The heart of the gospel

by Sinclair Ferguson

SINCLAIR FERGUSON

Dr Sinclair Ferguson is Professor of Systematic Theology at Westminster Theological Seminary. Since 2003 he has been serving mainly on the Seminary's Dallas campus, having previously taught on the Philadelphia campus from 1983 to 1998. He also serves as theologian-in-residence at Park Cities Presbyterian church, a six thousand member congregation in Dallas, and teaches there most weeks.

He is married to Dorothy and they have four grown-up children, three of whom are married and live in the UK. His pastoral experience has included serving as assistant minister to George B. Duncan in St George's-Tron church, Glasgow, where he also served as minister from 1998 to 2003. During the mid-1970s, he was minister on Unst, the most northerly inhabited island in Scotland. He is the author of some two dozen publications and writers regularly for magazines and journals.

The heart of the gospel

The subject of this lecture is the atonement, the heart of the gospel. In view of the fact that, in our seminary, a course of thirty-six lectures is devoted to the atonement, I've decided to narrow down our focus of attention virtually exclusively to the teaching of the apostle Paul, although I may refer to other parts of Scripture.

I want to begin by making a number of comments about the significance of the doctrine of the atonement and then to say three things: firstly, to paint in the basic context in which the apostle Paul thinks about Christ's atoning work; secondly, to bring to the surface what it is that Paul believes Christ accomplished on the cross; and thirdly, to make some response to four particular criticisms that are levelled increasingly at Paul's understanding of the gospel and the evangelical understanding of the atonement.

Why does it matter?

There are two reasons why it's important for us to study this theme. Firstly, because of its crucial biblical importance. The work of Christ lies at the heart of the gospel. The atonement, the death of Christ on the cross, lies at the centre of the gospel. In 1 Corinthians 15:1 and following, it belongs to what the apostle Paul describes as the 'first things' that are of supreme importance: 'Christ died for our sins according to the Scriptures.' Paul very obviously understands that simply to say 'Christ died' is not the gospel. The gospel is 'Christ died for our sins.' Any exposition of the Christian gospel, even one that places great sustaining emphasis on the dying of our Lord Jesus Christ, that doesn't specifically emphasise that he died for our sins, actually may use the language of gospel but has ceased to be gospel. The gospel is not simply the uninterpreted death of Jesus. There were two others who died almost simultaneously, on the right and left hand of Jesus. They are not of the essence of the gospel. Only because Jesus died for our sins, uniquely, is the message of the cross a message of good news.

What did Jesus think?

This is how our Lord Jesus himself understood his ministry. He came preaching the kingdom of God but at the epicentre of that message is that the Son of Man came to seek and to save that which was lost and does so by giving his life as ransom for many. Ransom in Scripture is always atonement language. Jesus says to the disciples on the road to Emmaus, and then to the apostles gathered together in Jerusalem, that it was not accidental but divinely necessary that the Christ should suffer and die and then be glorified. These words echo the fourth of the servant songs of Isaiah, that begins 'Who has believed our report and to whom has the arm of the LORD been revealed?' It describes how the Lord would be marred beyond human semblance. Jesus is echoing these words about the servant who will be disfigured, and yet, having been disfigured, will be exalted. He's saying 'It was therefore necessary for me to suffer and then enter into my glory, as the one who would be wounded for the transgression of others, bruised for the iniquities of others, chastised to bring divine shalom to others, and through whose beating men and women would ultimately, in the resurrection, be healed by the grace of God.'

What do the Gospels say?

Although the Gospels do not over-explicitly interpret the inner significance of the death of Jesus, they give somewhere between 30 and 40 per cent of their energies to expounding what happened in the last week of his life, and particularly what happened in the final twenty-four hours. As you read the passion narratives closely, you begin to see how they are teaching us what the inner significance of this man's death was. For example, in Luke chapter 23, he is declared by every single party involved in his crucifixion to be innocent of the charges and yet, according to the divine plan, is executed on the basis of two charges – blasphemy and treason – that just happen to be the two charges with which we are accused before the judgement seat of God. So in the Gospels we are invited to see how the atonement of Jesus Christ, in his death, lies at the very heart of the whole of the Bible's message. At the centre of the throne of glory is the Lamb who has been slain: a theme of tremendous biblical significance.

It's also a theme of enormous contemporary significance. Forty years ago, when I first became a Christian, I would imagine that an evangelical in the United Kingdom, and indeed almost anywhere in the world, would be marked by two distinctives; an absolute conviction of the infallibility and sufficiency of Holy Scripture and an absolute conviction that when Christ died on the cross, his death was a substitutionary, penal atonement. Now that, alas, is no longer the case. One of the sadnesses I see in much contemporary literature and contemporary speech about the atonement, that arise within the context of professing evangelicalism, is actually substantially identical to patterns of thinking that have emerged on several occasions over the last few hundred years in the Christian Church and which, without exception, have signalled the rise of anti-evangelicalism and liberalism. It's very important for us, in our contemporary climate, always to be asking this question as we read and listen: 'Is the heart of the gospel here in the teaching we are receiving?'

Most of our great hymns on the atonement, incidentally, express this principle. 'In my place condemned he stood, sealed my pardon with his blood, hallelujah, what a Saviour!' Now, that has never been the only aspect of the atoning work of Christ that the evangelical church has gloried in. Paradoxically, you may think, Isaac Watts' great hymn, 'When I survey the wondrous cross' is a hymn not so much about penal substitution as it is about the overwhelming influence on my life of the demonstration of the love of God in the gospel. But even 'When I survey the wondrous cross' forces me to ask how is it in the cross that the love of God is revealed? Why is it in the cross that the love of God in Jesus Christ is so overpowering to my soul? So I want to emphasise that neither in Scripture nor in evangelical preaching and hymnody has penal substitution been the only aspect of the atonement that the evangelical tradition has emphasised. But I think it's vital for us to see that unless penal substitution is present, all of those other aspects of the accomplishment of Jesus Christ in the atonement begin to fragment into so many emasculated pieces.

This is a subject of great contemporary significance and it is important for us always to remember that there is virtually nothing new in theology. There may be new voices and new packaging, but almost nothing is genuinely new. Much of the discussion on the atonement takes place at the so-called cutting edge of academic scholarship, which is often like a razor blade; it is intended to shave you clean but sometimes it causes the Christian church to bleed. There will be particular positions that some of you may identify with particular names but it would be invidious and probably taking advantage of the occasion if I named names. We are interested not in names but in truth and we must always come, together, subject to the truth of the gospel.

What did Paul teach?

I come to this with a number of presuppositions. The first is that the apostle Paul did in fact give us the thirteen letters in the New Testament that are ascribed to him. Secondly, that a close reading of the New Testament makes it abundantly clear that Paul thought of these letters as carrying exactly the same weight and divine authority as Old Testament Scripture. Thirdly, that this was recognised in the New Testament church: for example by the apostle Peter who refers to 'those difficult things in Paul's letters' and speaks of them as 'the Scriptures'. And fourthly, I presuppose that the apostle Paul, although he rarely alludes to it, did have a thorough knowledge of the story of the incarnation of our Lord Jesus, from his companionship with Luke and from the days he spent with Simon Peter. Don't you think it utterly unimaginable that Paul could be in the same room as Simon

Peter and not say 'Give me every last detail about our blessed Lord Jesus'?

Paul was deeply concerned about the atonement and understood not only that it was the heart of the gospel – 'I resolved to know nothing while I was with you but Jesus Christ and him crucified' – but was also deeply conscious that it was the cross that would constantly be under most attack. Take away the inner significance of the cross and you have taken away the inner significance of Christ and you have destroyed the gospel. So when he speaks to those who have misunderstood the cross, in his letter to the Galatians, he pronounces an anathema on anyone who preaches any other gospel. Paul is profoundly concerned in his letters about two different kinds of attack on the gospel. One comes from those who deny the truth of Christ's atonement; and the other from those who regard the truth of Christ's atonement as a matter of secondary consideration, open to discussion. There is both a straightforward denial of the atonement and a decentralising of the atonement. For Paul, both of these are inherently destructive of the gospel.

Paul's understanding of the atonement

For Paul, the atonement is not monolithic. There's not just one aspect to what Christ did on the cross. If I can put it into popular jargon, on the cross our Lord Jesus was multi-tasking and it's important for us to recognise that. So for example in Romans, Paul speaks about what happened on the cross as propitiation, expiation, redemption, reconciliation and so on. He understands there is something being effected in the death of Christ that is multi-levelled in its ability to deal with the multi-faceted consequences of Adam's fall and our sin. But for the apostle Paul there is a basic understanding that undergirds everything that he has to say. It's particularly obvious in Romans 5:12-21 and 1 Corinthians 15:20-28 and 45-49. These are two dense passages. Let me highlight what Paul's drivers are.

Adam and Christ

Paul understands that there is a sense in which God has dealt with the whole of humanity through two single historical figures: Adam, whom he describes in 1 Corinthians 15 as 'the first man' as well as 'the first Adam'; and the Lord Jesus Christ, whom he describes as 'the second man' and 'the last Adam'. It's that description that helps us to understand the almost cosmic proportions of Paul's understanding of the significance of Jesus Christ. He understands by calling the Lord Jesus 'the second man' that there has been no man since Adam who fulfils the role that the Lord Jesus fulfils. By calling him 'the last Adam' Paul underlines for us that there cannot be any other after Christ who also fulfils this role. His over-arching consideration is that when God created the human race, he created it with a representative head and leader, a father, and as things went with that representative head, so things have gone with the whole of humanity. This is his teaching, for example, in Romans chapter 5, where he emphasises that the one man, Adam, sinned and his one act of disobedience led to death passing upon all, because the whole of human-ity shared in Adam's sin and fell under Adam's judgement. He was a rep-resentative figure as well as being the root of the whole of humanity.

It's very clear, in Romans 5 and in 1 Corinthians 15 as well as else-where, that the apostle Paul thought of Adam as a historical figure. He says this in order to help us understand the significance of our Lord Jesus Christ. How is it that the action of one individual can have such a radical effect on multitudes of individuals? Because our Lord Jesus Christ is not, as the older writers used to say, simply a private figure. The Lord Jesus Christ is the second man, he's the second one like Adam, and he is the last Adam, and God is doing something in the Lord Jesus Christ in order to reverse everything that was accomplished by the first man, Adam. As Paul looks back upon the garden of Eden, he recog-nises that the first man, Adam, by his one act of disobedience, brought down the whole of the created order in catastrophe. The glory of the atoning work in the death and resurrection of Jesus, the last Adam, is that he comes to undo what the first Adam had done and to accom-plish what he failed to do. Jesus comes to bear the judgement of God upon all that the sin of the first man, Adam, had brought into being and, declared to be the Son of God in the power of his resurrection, to become the last Adam. In becoming the last Adam, he became the first man of the new creation whose resurrection, as Paul says in 1 Corinthians 15, is the guarantee of the resurrection of us all. When by faith through the Spirit we are united to this second man and last Adam, all that has been lost in Adam is restored in Jesus Christ for believers.

What happened because of Adam's sin that our Lord Jesus Christ needs to repair? The Early Fathers of the Christian church, through the first five centuries (and the theme reappears in the Reformation and in different ways in the evangelical tradition) used an expression to encapsulate their understanding of the atonement. They said that the unassumed is the unhealed, the unredeemed. They understood that if the Lord Jesus was to make atonement for our sin, then everything that was involved in that sin and its consequences, somehow or another, would need to be placed upon his shoulders, so that he might bear the consequences of our sin and in his humanity do for us what we have failed to do. In the power of his resurrection, Jesus went back to heaven and said, 'Father, now give me the Holy Spirit you promised, that we may effect in men and women all that I have accomplished in my incarnation and death and resurrection, assuming their loss in order to share with them my gain.'

What have we lost?

Paul has different ways of describing the plight of men and women. Here are five principles that run particularly through his letters to the Romans and Ephesians.

Children of wrath

Sin brings us under guilt, and guilt under the wrath of God; that's what Romans 1:18 and Romans 3:19,20 are all about. Paul, the Jewish convert, says about himself and the Gentile Ephesians, 'We were all by nature children of wrath, whether Jew or Gentile …' Whether we are Jew or Gentile, it makes no difference whatsoever to the transition that needs to take place for us in Jesus Christ and in us by God's grace: we all need to be transitioned from wrath to grace.

Alienation

Because of that, secondly, we are alienated from God. Paul emphasises, for example in 1 Thessalonians, that if we remain alienated from

God in this life, we will be alienated by the very presence of God in the life to come. It's just possible that the preposition he uses there not only signifies that we have been alienated *from* the presence of God but it will be the very presence of God that will speak to us; we will be alienated *by* that holy presence of God.

Bondage

Thirdly, there is bondage in sin and the ways of the world, Ephesians 2:1-3. There is a twofold bondage to be dealt with; there is my bondage under sin's dominion and there is my enslavement to Satan's power.

Children of Satan

Fourthly, I am not only by nature a child of wrath; I am by nature a child of Satan, as the apostle of love, John, underscores in his first letter.

Disintegration

Fifthly, there is disintegration in death. 'The wages of sin is death' – the disintegration of that which God originally made as a glorious unity. My being as spirit and my being as body, that God made a most glorious unity, has been fractured by sin; sin has brought disintegration into my life. The end of that disintegration is the horror of death.

This is what Adam brought into the world – his guilt, hiding from God; his alienation, ashamed to be with God; his bondage in sin, his awful enslavement to Satan, his promised disintegration in death. Adam was created to have dominion over the earth, and it appears from the early chapters of Genesis that God gave him a start. He put him in a garden and he said 'Now turn the whole world into a garden.' He made him for fellowship with himself. 'Be like me,' he says, 'I create in six days and then I rest. I give you six days and then you rest. I have dominion over the whole cosmos. You have dominion over the earth. I am a creating God. Go and create in marvellous ways. I'm a naming God, go and name.' And because of Adam's supreme position, when he falls, the cosmos falls with him.

The curse of Genesis chapter 2 falls not simply on the serpent, the woman and the man, but on the earth. Paul says in Romans chapter 8:20 that this world has been subjected to bondage, to decay. The whole cosmos fell under the curse. This is my plight: child of wrath, guilty, alienated from God, bound in sin, enslaved to Satan, disintegrating in death and living in a world that is subjected to the decay of a cosmic curse.

How does Christ make atonement?

This leads us to the second thing that Paul expounds against that background. If this is the basic context for the atonement, what is the transaction effected in the atonement? The biblical perspective is very simple. God looks for a man; but because we're all under the curse there is no man who can arise with healing in his wings. So there is, dare we call it, a community plan on the part of the Father, Son and Holy Spirit. The Son is sent into the world to bear our humanity, to become the second Adam. What Jesus came to do was to undo what Adam did. The second man does what Adam failed to do: he lives a life of wholesome obedience to his Father. The second Adam bears the consequences of what Adam the first did and so he necessarily comes under the judgement and wrath of God.

All authority

Thirdly, the second man effects what Adam was called to accomplish but failed to accomplish – the subduing of the whole world under his feet. Matthew's gospel, the gospel of the king, announces the king has come: 'Where is he who was born king of the Jews?' It ends with our Lord's words – speaking as the second man and the last Adam – 'All authority in heaven and earth is now mine.' That's the language of the opening chapters of Genesis: 'Adam, all authority in the heavens and in the earth is yours.' 'Therefore,' Jesus says, 'now that all that authority has been restored by me, in me, for me, through me, go and have dominion to the ends of the earth and to the ends of the ages and bring in the kingdom.'

The obedience of Christ

In Philippians 2:5-11, Paul describes our Lord Jesus Christ almost as though he were Adam in reverse. Although he was in 'very nature

God,' he didn't count equality with God a thing to be held on to or to take advantage of, unlike Adam who grasped for it. 'But (he) made himself of nothing, taking the very nature of a servant ... and ... he humbled himself and' (unlike Adam the first) Adam the second 'became obedient unto death.'

What is the antithesis to Adam's sin in Romans 5:12-21? It's the obedience of the one man, Jesus Christ, unto death. The over-arching principle Paul uses to help us to understand what Christ accomplishes is that, in the whole course of his life, as the new Adam, as the divinely provided substitute for us, Jesus does what Adam the first failed to do. It is that context of a whole life of happy obedience to his heavenly Father, not least happy obedience in those areas that must have gone completely against the instinct of holy humanity: holy humanity can never naturally desire to experience what it means to cry out 'My God, why have you forsaken me?' As the Father had asked Adam in the garden of Eden, 'Don't eat from the fruit of that tree, simply because I'm asking you; trust me for no other reason than that I am your God', so in the garden of Gethesemane, as Jesus faces Calvary, the Father is saying to him, 'Trust me even though what I'm asking you to do goes against every last instinct in your being. Be obedient unto death, my Son.' We've got this glorious picture of all that Adam failed to do being accomplished by our Lord Jesus Christ. Within that whole context, Jesus then deals with the nature, the implications and the consequence of our sin.

How anyone in their right mind can read the letter of Paul to the Romans and fail to understand the gospel is almost beyond imagination. Those who do, always marginalise what Paul has to say about the wrath of God. But his gospel is that our Lord Jesus Christ, in his godliness and perfect righteousness, is presented by the God of wrath on the cross of Calvary as a propitiation, in fulfilment of the mutual commitment of the Father and the Son to save sinners. Our Lord Jesus Christ becomes what Paul calls a propitiation for our sins. It doesn't matter very much at all whether we translate the Greek word as 'the mercy seat' as it often appears in the Septuagint version of the Old Testament, or whether we translate it as it almost always was understood in the Greek world to which Paul belonged, as a propitiatory sacrifice that dealt with the wrath of God. The sheer genius of this in the teaching of the New Testament is that it was just as the heavenly Father was pouring out his wrath upon his Son as representative and substitute for sinners, it was then that he loved his Son in our flesh to a degree that had been impossible. He could love his Son as the eternal one for all eternity but remember how Jesus puts it in John 10:17 – 'The reason the Father loves me is because I lay down my life.' I wish people who so demean the wrath of God would understand that they're simultaneously demeaning the love of God for his Son. It's precisely in the outpouring of his wrath upon his Son that the Father loves his Son in our flesh, because he's been willing to be obedient to death, even the death of the cross.

Reconciliation

There is propitiation, Romans 3:21 following. There is reconciliation, says the apostle: 'We preach the gospel of reconciliation' – Romans 5:10 and 2 Corinthians 5:19-21. God was in Christ reconciling the world to himself, not counting men's trespasses against them. I can almost hear people say, 'That's what I mean when I say that God is not a God of wrath. He doesn't count men's trespasses against them.' I want to say, in the name of God, read on. Because if you do, the only thing you will be able to do, as indeed some contemporary scholars have done, is to say that 2 Corinthians 5:21 is actually a statement more about the apostle Paul than it is about the work of Jesus on the cross. Paul isn't saying God doesn't count men's sins, he's saying God doesn't count men's sins against them *because* he made him to be sin for us who knew no sin, in order that we all might become in him the righteousness of God. There is propitiation in Christ, there's reconciliation in Christ, and we are in sin's foul bondage and there is redemption in Christ. Christ, our Passover lamb, is sacrificed for us. Because of his sacrifice we are set free from the dominion of sin.

Victory in the death of Christ

We have come under the bondage of the evil one; we are not only children of wrath, we are the children of the serpent. In his dying for our sins as an atonement and rising from the grave, Jesus leaves behind

a defeated enemy. The question is, how does the death of Jesus defeat
Satan? The death of Jesus defeats Satan because it clears us of guilt. It
is guilt that gives Satan a hold over us. Part of his power is in black-
mailing the guilty, and those whose guilt has been expunged are free
from his power. There is no liberation from the power of Satan unless
there is propitiation that deals with our fear of the wrath of God, and
expiation of our guilt.

Freedom from the curse

Sometimes scholars say, 'He's talking about the curse of the broken
Mosaic law.' That may be included, but what Paul's actually speaking
about is the curse that is the antithesis of the blessing, promised not to
Moses but promised through Abraham, the blessing that releases us
from an older curse than the curse of the law of Moses, that releases
us from the curse of the garden of Eden. Jesus became a curse for us
in order that we might receive the blessing of God. Blessing is the
word that comes from the original creation; God saw that everything
was good and he rested and so he blessed the whole of his creation
week by blessing the last day of it. Everything was blessed and everything fell under the curse. Jesus falls under the curse but as he rises
from underneath that curse, he rises as a new man in resurrection
power and becomes the first man of the new age who has dominion
over all the earth. As the Son of Man, he shares that dominion, that
freedom from the curse, with all who trust in him.

So what are the criticisms of penal substitution?

1:    'The doctrine of penal substitution is a relatively new doctrine in
      the history of the entire church.'

Anyone who says that does not understand the history of theology. It
is often said that the Early Fathers really believed that Jesus paid a
ransom to Satan: a small number of them did believe that. But not
even those who believed that Christ's ransom was paid to Satan were
ignorant of the fact that the work of Jesus Christ was a propitiation
that dealt with the wrath of God. That's simply a false and ignorant
use of the history of the Christian Church – and it would be

corrected by a good reading of the Fathers of the Christian Church, incidentally.

2: 'Penal substitution distorts the central gospel message of the love of God.'

One of the things we've been seeing in the New Testament's understanding of the atonement is that penal substitution under the wrath of God is the supreme demonstration of the love of God. Paul says, 'Where is the love of God demonstrated? In that while we were yet sinners, Christ died for the ungodly by bearing the wrath of God that falls on all ungodliness.' Christ bore the wrath of a Father … The wrath of God is not God flying off the handle. In expressing that holy wrath, the Father's heart was simultaneously drawn out towards his Son, like a father standing on the touchline as his son scores the winning goal in the FA Cup Final, his chest swelling with pride, thinking 'That's my boy!'

3: 'The doctrine of penal substitution implies the doctrine of a double imputation; our sins imputed to Christ, Christ's righteousness imputed to us.'

Very scholarly men these days are saying that is an impossibility for one simple reason: righteousness is an attribute and an attribute cannot be imputed to somebody else. They say, 'We want to say that Christ did die in some sense for our sins but there is no double imputation.' I want you to see that goes inevitably to its logical conclusion – my sin is my attribute, and if this righteousness of Jesus Christ cannot become mine, then my sin cannot become his. There is a logic that works here that destroys not just part of the traditional understanding of the gospel but the whole possibility of all imputation.

4: 'These are simply so many theories of the atonement, and they are just metaphors. We shouldn't raise one of those metaphors to be the controlling metaphor.'

That entirely reverses biblical thinking. All of these so-called metaphors of the Bible were given by God in revelation precisely in order to explain to us what his Son was going to do. The fallacy here is the assumption that men are taking man-made metaphors in order to describe something that is divinely transcendent. In fact, the truth is almost the reverse. God is creating pictures of what happens transcendentally to explain to human beings so that they may understand spiritually.

The old gospel

I read a book as a young Christian, written by a well-known minister in London. It was a book of overwhelming power. It portrayed a Jesus whom to follow was the most glorious adventure in life. But I felt, even as a youngster, there was something not quite right here. I didn't know then always to ask the question, 'What is he not saying?' I later came to understand that he denied the reality of the wrath of God, of penal substitution. It was what people used to call liberal theology, a God without wrath, a Christ without a cross, a Christian life without sacrifice. I read another book in recent months that spoke similarly of a wonderful Jesus whom to follow was the greatest adventure in life. But the word I looked for in the book occurred very rarely and then it was usually to sideline it. It was the word 'sin' and its cousin, the word 'wrath.' Was it not once said by a heavenly being, 'You shall call his name "Jesus" because supremely among all other things he comes to do, he comes to save his people from their sins'? I know people call that the old gospel but it's so old that you find it's the gospel of the Bible.

The Addresses

JOE STOWELL

Joe Stowell serves as a teaching pastor at Harvest Bible Chapel. Harvest is a thriving Christian fellowship of nearly eight thousand that meets on three campuses across the northwest suburbs of Chicago. Before coming to Harvest in March 2005, Joe served as the seventh president of Moody Bible Institute where he led that multi-faceted ministry for eighteen years.

His prevailing passions are to express the heart of the gospel by keeping Christ pre-eminent in all of life; to embrace the body of Christ across colour and class distinctions, and to focus attention on ministry needs in the urban centres, as well as global needs and trends.

An internationally recognised conference speaker and author, Joe has written numerous books, including *Simply Jesus, Strength for the Journey*, and his most recent, *The Final Question of Jesus*. He is also heard weekdays on the award-winning radio Bible teaching programme, 'Proclaim!'

Joe is a graduate of Cedarville University and Dallas Theological seminary, and was honoured with a doctor of divinity degree from the

Masters' College in 1987. Joe and his wife Martie are the parents of three adult children and have ten grandchildren. They make their home in suburban Chicago.

Inside-out living (1)

Introduction

A couple of weeks ago my wife Martie went to visit her sister in Michigan for a week, leaving me home alone. You can imagine what the house looked like the day before she was coming back. Suddenly I realised that either she could walk in the door and clean it up herself or I could clean it up. I decided to clean it up and I went to the kitchen, cleaned the pots and pans and put the dishes in the dishwasher. I straightened up all the magazines and newspapers I'd left all over. I even made the bed. I picked up my dirty socks, I got everything. When Martie walked in the house, it was beautiful. She looked at me. 'Joe, the house is so beautiful. Why have you done this?' And I looked at her, with all the depth of meaning that I could muster and said, 'Because I am committed to the institution of marriage, that is why.' And she swooned.

Actually I didn't say that. I said to her, 'Martie, you need to know how much I love you.' Behind all of that was a depth of gratitude in my heart for the years which she's spent with me. When I was busy in the ministry, she cared so well for our kids and helped to rear them and what a coach and an encouragement she has been. I owe so much to Martie: it was a delight for me to clean the house as an expression of love to her.

If Jesus were to turn to you right now and say, 'Why are you following me?' I wonder if you would look him right in the eyes, with all the depth of heart you could muster and say, 'I am committed to Christianity.'

A lot of us live like that. Our Christianity is all about the rules, the traditions, the doctrines, the system, the rituals, the hoops we jump through. I've come all the way from Chicago to tell you that authentic Christianity is not a duty, it's not about being committed to Christianity. Authentic Christianity is about devotion to Jesus Christ and doing all that we do because we love him, out of deep hearts of gratitude.

Here's a big warning; if your Christianity becomes simply duty, simply not wanting to get caught, being afraid of the consequences, doing what everybody tells you to do, your Christianity will soon become burdensome and boring and when the tempter comes, it will be really easy to bail out. But if your Christianity is all about a deep loving devotion to a Saviour not to a system, to a relationship not to a set of rituals, your heart will be liberated and you will know the joy that Jesus intended you to have.

The new covenant

Jesus Christ paid a great price for your Christianity not to be a matter of duty but of devotion. And that great price was articulated in the upper room, when he lifted the cup and he said this, 'This cup is the new covenant in my blood.' When he said that, the disciples perked up their ears and their hearts. Because a long time ago, the prophet Jeremiah had promised that the day would come when the new covenant would be engaged.

Turn to Jeremiah chapter 31. The prophet Jeremiah says, 'Behold'. This is the Hebrew word for 'Take note, listen to this.' "'Behold, the days are coming," declares the Lord, "when I will make a new covenant with the house of Israel and with the house of Judah.'"

What I would like to do, first of all, is land on that word 'new'. That's a very compelling word. I love new things. You know the seductive smell of a new car? Who wouldn't drain thousands of pounds just to be able to have the smell of a new car? Unfortunately it has a way of then becoming old. Martie and I had this Chevvy we used to drive around in. In America we have these big church dinners where everybody bakes a little stuff and brings it along. She had baked this big ham and on the floor was this ham with all the gravy. I hit the brakes a little too abruptly and the ham gravy was everywhere. The new smell of that car was gone forever and that's just the way things happen in this world.

When you were born you got a new body; how exciting was that? And when you were thirty your metabolism changed a little bit, started bulking up. When you were forty, your arms weren't long enough to read any more. I remember going to a fiftieth birthday party with a friend of mine and his wife had these little napkins that said, 'Of all the things I've lost, I miss my mind the most.' By the time you're sixty your body's falling apart. You bend over to pick something up and you stay down there to see what else you can get done on the trip. The things that are new have a way of becoming old, don't they?

Here's the really good news; when God talks about a new covenant, he is speaking of a much larger picture. The theme of this week is the glory of the gospel. I hope that you don't think that the gospel is 'John 3:16, thank you. Nail it on a friend and get them saved and there's the gospel.' I hope you don't think that the gospel is just about hell cancelled and heaven guaranteed. The gospel is big, wide and deep. The good news of Jesus Christ stretches beyond just what happened at the cross. Praise God for the cross but it is so much more life-transforming than that. And when we read here the prophet Jeremiah saying, 'Behold ... I will make a new covenant', it's a clue that God is into a far different kind of new.

Turn quickly to Revelation chapter 21. John says, 'I saw a new heaven and a new earth; for the first heaven and the first earth passed away.' All of the world, everything we live in, is a part of a decaying, decadent, fallen place where the new is always eroding to the old. He says:

> ... there was no longer any sea. And I saw the holy city, new Jerusalem, coming down out of heaven from God, made ready as a bride adorned for her husband. And I heard a loud voice from the throne, saying, 'Behold, the tabernacle of God is among men and He will dwell

among them and they shall be His people and God Himself will be among them.

I love this because this old fallen broken world that we live in is a very disappointing place. So often our hearts are broken under the weight of the fallenness of this place. Is there any follower of Jesus Christ that loves these next words? 'He will wipe away every tear from their eyes; and there will no longer be any death; there will no longer be any mourning, or crying, or pain; the first things have passed away. And He who sits on the throne said, "Behold, I am making all things new."'

When he makes something new, it is above and beyond the decaying decadent world in which we live. I love it when God talks about his kind of new. If you belong to Jesus Christ, you are a part of an emerging new culture. This gives me great hope because I live in a world that keeps telling me, 'You're so retro as a Christian, you're so old-fashioned. Why don't you get a life?' I'm here to say, 'Get a biblical life because everything in this world is passing away and those who are in Jesus Christ are not retro. If you are in him, you are part of an emerging newness that will never grow old throughout all of eternity.' So when your world tells you, 'You're so retro, you're so old-fashioned' just look at them and say, 'Could I welcome you to all that is new?' See how that goes.

Definitions of covenant

A binding agreement

So when I read the prophet saying that there is a new covenant, my heart springs to listen. He said, 'Behold the days are coming when I will make a new covenant.' Let's camp on this word covenant for a minute, because it is full of such encouragement to us. A covenant in the Old Testament was more than an agreement. When the word covenant is used in the Old Testament, it is about a binding agreement. You can shake hands with somebody, walk away and forget about it but you can't sign a deal with the estate agent and have a contract and walk away from it because it is a binding agreement. All through the Old Testament this is a very common word for God's binding agreements with his people. You've got the covenant he made with Adam, the covenant he made with Abraham, the covenant he made with Moses; the binding agreement he made with David that David's throne would last forever and some day the King of Kings, Jesus himself, would sit on the Davidic throne. It's a very common theme through the Old Testament that God is a God of binding agreements with his people.

You need to know it's just not an agreement, it's something you can trust in. Can you make an agreement and trust somebody? There's not a lot of people in this world you can trust. But when God makes a binding agreement with you, he has bound himself to it and he is faithful and just to carry it out. So this new covenant is a binding agreement.

Abundant favour

In that day, covenants were made between equals and often those were agreements of equality but when a superior made a covenant with a lesser person, it was always that the superior was going to pour out abundant favour on the lesser person. So is this an agreement between a greater and a lesser? The Almighty God is making a binding agreement with you: this is the superior to the lesser. Which means that in this binding agreement, God is going to be pouring out abundant favour upon you.

The third aspect of covenants is that some of God's covenants with his people were conditional, like the Mosaic covenant. But some of them were unconditional: they didn't depend on you or how you behaved. Read through this new covenant in Jeremiah: God is saying "I will.' Five times it says, 'I will ... I will ... I will ... I will ... I will.' This is an unconditional covenant. Think of God making a binding agreement with you, where he's going to pour out his favour on you and it is unconditional. It will happen, if you are a part of the new covenant. Think about how wonderful that is and that's exactly what the prophet Jeremiah is proclaiming, 'Behold the days are coming when I will make a new covenant.'

By the way, we might want to note that at the end of verse 31 he says, 'I will make a new covenant with the house of Israel and with the house of Judah.' You say, 'I'm not Jewish, is that a problem?' When Jesus stood at the last supper and said, 'This cup is the new covenant in my blood,' how extensive was that? It's by the marvellous grace of God that he has grafted us into this marvellous privilege through the shedding of his blood, the beginning of the new covenant: so this is about you.

The old covenant

Then he contrasts the new covenant with the old covenant, verse 32. But it will be 'not like the covenant which I made with their fathers in the day I took them by the hand to bring them out of the land of Egypt, My covenant which they broke, although I was a husband to them.' He's speaking here of the Mosaic covenant, the covenant of the law. We need to talk about that for a minute because a lot of us have this crazy thought about the old covenant of the law. Do you ever think, 'I'm so glad I'm not an Old Testament person, back under the pressure of the law. Now we're in the New Testament, we live under grace, isn't that a wonderful thing?' And the law is trashed. I want you to know that all through the New Testament, the law is revered. The law of Moses was God's gift of grace to his people, because the law averts moral and civic chaos. Here the children of Israel were going into the land of Canaan and as they moved into this pagan land, where there was anarchy in every town, where the highest point of religious allegiance was to sacrifice your newborn child to gods of wood and stone – how would they be different? How would they avert the moral and civic chaos of a pagan land like Canaan? They would have the law of God. That's why Romans chapter 7:12 says, 'The law is holy and righteous and good.'

The world works better when the laws of God are in place: when we don't lie to each other and don't sleep with each others' wives and don't steal and don't covet what each other has, when we don't murder each other. It's just a better world like that. I speak for America, that's trying to chuck out all the laws, as though life would be better without them. Life would not be better without them. You say, 'I don't like all that law stuff like an eye for an eye and a tooth for a tooth.' Do you realise that that was the grace of God? Because when we do damage to each other, it tends to escalate. It's like you said something bad to me, I say something bad to you louder and you hit me back and then I look for a club and then you look for a knife. When we offend each other, it escalates. We have to recognise that the old covenant was not a mistake of God. It was for a very important season but it had one tragic flaw, compared to the new covenant.

Where was the law of God in the old covenant? On tablets of stone. The law of the Old Testament was external. It was not an internal thing: it was conformity to a list of rules on the outside. Israel did not have a heart for the law because it was external. Someone is watching. You will be in trouble. You'll be stoned outside the city gates. And it was all this external, consequential and nothing inside.

Maybe we can understand it like this; in the States we have stop lights everywhere. They avert moral chaos and civic anarchy. Can you imagine a world without stop lights or roundabouts? We'd be crashing into each other, dragging people out of the cars. I think stop lights are a really good idea because they avert moral chaos but I do not have a heart for stop lights. It was just like that with Israel and while it was important for that season of travelling in this pagan land, God needed something better. God needed something that wasn't just external.

The glory of the Gospel

I want you to read the four elements of this new covenant that Jesus brings in, the glory of the gospel in the new covenant and read the contrast. '"But this is the covenant which I will make with the house of Israel after those days" (verse 33) declares the Lord. "I will put my law within them, it will be not external but it will be internal."' There will be something going on on the inside. It is no longer external but it is internal. 'I will write it on their hearts and I will be their God and they shall be my people.'

In the old covenant of the law, there was no intimacy with God. In the text we read that God said that Israel broke the covenant 'even though I was a husband to them'. That's intimate? Not really: back in those days husbands were patriarchal, they led the clan. God was a

provider, a protector of everybody in the Old Testament. How intimate is it when you can't approach him? Remember the book of
Leviticus; only the high priest could approach God and if you dared
enter his presence, you would die. Intimacy was not a part of it. But
then he says, the day is coming '... on their heart I will write it; and I
will be their God and they shall be my people.'

Verse 34, 'They shall not teach again, each man his neighbour and
each man his brother, saying, "Know the Lord."' The old covenant was
instructional, it kept reminding people about God. The new covenant
is instinctive. Are you getting the contrast now? It is not external, it is
internal. It is not patriarchal, it is intimate. The old covenant was
instructional, the new covenant is instinctive. You will instinctively
know God from the inside out.

I love this 'For in the new covenant, I will forgive their inequity
and their sin, I will remember no more.' You're saying, 'In the old
covenant, they had ways to deal with sin.' Absolutely. But it was a big
deal. You sinned, you had to get a lamb, shed its blood and you were
absolved of your sins. Then the next time you sinned, what did you
have to do again? There was that constant repetitive need because
under the old covenant, you are so aware of your failure and there is
no release.

Then God says that the day is coming under the new covenant
where he will, once and for all, forgive sins and will remember them
no more. Whereas you have periodic restoration under the Old
Testament, under the new covenant you are declared innocent before
God, all of your sins covered under his matchless blood. This is the
promise.

Internal or external?

It's important for us to stop and ask ourselves one very important
question. Is my Christianity characterised by old covenant external,
law-keeping systems of external governance? Or have I come to
know the joy of the liberty of the new covenant in Jesus Christ? I'm
greatly concerned about how often we slide back into externalised
forms of Christianity. We're just about the habits and the rituals and

it's about not wanting to get caught and what would the consequences be. If you live in an externalised, systematised religion, it makes for proud grumpy old saints. What happened to the freshness, the openness, the devotion, the love, the celebration?

Jesus was the bringer of the new covenant. All through the gospels, we see old covenant rule-keeper/new covenant Jesus experiences taking place. I think my favourite one is in Luke chapter 7. It's about an old covenant rule-keeper; Simon the Pharisee. He's the good person in this story, the best guy in town. He knew all the rules, he kept them. Luke says that this old covenant rule-keeper, Simon the Pharisee, invited Jesus to dinner.

The Pharisee and the prostitute

Jesus' push back on people was not for the least and the lame and the losers and the marginalised but it was always these religious folks. I mean that ought to be a clue right there, for all of us who are lost in rule-keeping, that Jesus' biggest push back was against the rule-keepers. I'm for the biblical rules but not for the rules we make up and put on.

Jesus goes to dinner with a rule-keeper and Luke says, 'There was a woman in town who was a sinner.' He uses the Greek word for immoral sin, so here's a woman who at best is openly immoral, at worst and most probably the town prostitute. Luke does this all the time through his gospel, he puts the worst person with the best person and sticks Jesus in the middle.

Jesus goes to the rule-keeper's house. The guy's a little chagrined because Jesus and these old covenant rule-keepers weren't getting along well. Maybe he was embarrassed that, at the next Pharisees' convention in Jerusalem, he'd have to tell people he had Jesus come over. So he didn't kiss Jesus, which was a normal welcoming, at the door. Servants didn't wash Jesus' feet and this old covenant rule-keeper kept his distance by not anointing Jesus as the guest of honour.

In those days, this dinner would have been a major community event, held out in the courtyard of the palatial home of the Pharisee. They left the doors open, and people who weren't invited to eat could come and stand around the edges of the room, so it wasn't unusual that this woman was there. But what was unusual, as she stood in the margins of this dining-room, was that she stepped from the crowd and made her way to Jesus. And when this woman, probably the town prostitute, began walking, all the servants stopped and the shuffling of the wine glasses and the passing of the plates all stopped as well. This is not a big town, everybody knows who this woman is. I bet some of these guests are going, 'She's going to tell on me.'

She makes her way to Jesus. Think about how intimidating that is, in the presence of the one who has publicly condemned her on the streets. She has the unintimidated courage to reach Jesus in this dinner. She stands behind him as he reclined and in humility, falls down and begins weeping, pouring out her tears. Then she takes a vial of alabaster and pours it out in an act of sacrificial worship. She lets down her hair and wipes his feet and worships Jesus Christ, with unintimidated courage, in the most intimidating environment possible.

Simon the rule-keeper, he's thinking, 'This night is not turning out the way I thought it would.' He's got a big problem. His rules don't have space for this. So he says to himself, in his mind, 'Jesus is not who he claims to be. He is clearly not a prophet because if he were a prophet, he would know what kind of woman this woman was and not permit her to do this to him.' In that day, part of a prophet's credentials would be that they had a special intuition. He's saying, 'Jesus ought to know better than this.'

I love what Jesus does next. Jesus says, 'Simon, you don't think I'm a prophet. I just read your mind.' He answers his mental objection and tells this story. He says that there is someone who has been five hundred denarii in debt and he is forgiven and someone is fifty denarii in debt and he is forgiven. Who will love more? Since it's not rocket science, Simon gets it right. He says, 'Obviously the person who is forgiven more, will love more.' Then Jesus says, 'You did not anoint my head or wash my feet or kiss me when I came. This woman, since she has come, has not stopped pouring out adoration and devotion and affection to me.' Then he says why. He says, 'Simon, those who are forgiven much, love much.'

We're beginning to see this whole sense of the contrast of the new covenant and the old covenant. Those who are rule-keepers don't love much, those who are forgiven much, love much. And he says something very stinging to Simon: 'Simon, those who are forgiven little, love little.' Do you think that he is saying, "Simon, you're a good guy. You don't need to be forgiven much. I don't expect you to love me much"? That is not what he is saying to Simon.

Jesus knows what a deep sinner Simon really is. Jesus is saying, 'Simon, you don't think you need to be forgiven much, that's why you don't love me much.' That's the sting in the tail. We have a lot of good people in this tent tonight and if you're not careful, you won't think that you're a part of the 'forgiven much'. Jesus didn't die for nice people, all right? He didn't come and die for you because you are so good and keep all the rules. He died for us because we were deeply offensive to him in our sins. In fact the better you get, the worse you might become because you might start feeling good about yourself. The stealthy sin of pride could take over your life and you could put Jesus at a distance because now it's all about you.

Jesus died for me because I was born in sin and I have sinned and I'm horribly offensive to him. It is a new covenant thought that we are in that sub-culture of people called the 'forgiven much'. And when you are in that understanding, you will love much and you will serve, worship and adore him, out of a heart of devotion and not just do it because you're committed to Christianity. That's the heart of the new covenant.

At the Moody Bible Institute in Chicago, every year, for years and years, we've had this Founders' week. People come from all over America to fill up the great Moody church in Chicago. The Brooklyn Tabernacle choir were singing that night. Here are these one hundred and eighty people who've come from Brooklyn to Chicago to sing for us and they're not professional singers. These are crack addicts and former prostitutes who have been redeemed.

I'll never forget the moment, when the lights went down and the spotlight hit the choir and they sang their first great song of the glory of the redeeming work of Jesus Christ. I saw something I'd never seen in a choir before. As they began to sing, the spots were catching the glistening tears that were running down the cheeks of those singing the glory of the gospel in Jesus Christ. I felt cheated because I'm a lifer. I was saved when I was six, so I was saved from things like biting my sister and not picking up my toys. Sometimes it's hard for us lifers to get a grip on how much we've been forgiven for. And in the midst of my feeling cheated, it was as though the Holy Spirit began to work me over and said, 'Joe, did you ever think of where you might be, if I had not rescued you at six? Did you ever think of where your lust might have taken you, if my Spirit hadn't been bringing along self-control? Have you ever thought about where your greed would have taken you, if I hadn't been schooling you in generosity? Where your self-centredness would have taken you if I had not been teaching you the love of others? Did you ever?' Then it dawned on me; thank God I am among the forgiven much. I owe such a debt and so do you. It's because Jesus lifted that cup and said, 'Now is the time. Behold, this is the new covenant in my blood.' That is the glory of the gospel.

Inside-out living (2)

Introduction

It had been a good few days for Christ and his disciples. The crowds had met him and thrown their cloaks in the way, as though they were welcoming a victorious conqueror, and waved the palm branches and shouted 'Hosanna'. Jesus had gone into the temple and chased out the thieves, those folk in the temple who were ripping off the pilgrims by charging exorbitant prices for sacrifices. I think the disciples probably enjoyed watching him do those things but the best was yet to come. They go into that upper room and sit down: one of the final moments with Jesus Christ.

Then he lifted the cup and according to Luke 22:20 he said, 'This cup ... is the new covenant in my blood.' There had to be a buzz in the room because these guys had laboured long under the old system. Over the years, the religious establishment had turned it into a system of rule-keepers watching rule-keepers and rule-keepers judging non-rule-keepers; a system so complex, with so many laws, that they had to have religious lawyers to adjudicate the system. These men all knew what the prophet Jeremiah had said: 'Behold, the days are coming ... when I will make a new covenant.' The new covenant would be internal and intimate. Think what it meant for these men to hear that announcement on that day: the day was coming when the burden of the old system would be lifted and their relationship with God would be an inside-out thing. Joy must have swept through that room when they heard 'this cup is the new covenant in my blood'.

Luke doesn't give us what John gives us; John gives us what we call the Upper Room Discourse, where Jesus begins to teach them about the things that are to come. He is teaching them the roll-out of the covenant. The old covenant was external, the new covenant would be internal. Under the old covenant God was present with his people and yet distant, veiled behind the veils of the temple in the Holy of Holies, accessible only through the high priest. But in the new covenant there would be intimacy with God.

Performance-based Christianity

All you 'star chart' followers of Jesus Christ, all you performance-based Christians, have a problem. We forget how much we need Christ, we forget about grace, because we think we're so good. It reminds me of one of my favourite nursery rhymes.

> Little Jack Horner sat in a corner eating his Christmas pie
> He stuck in his thumb and pulled out a plum
> (Here's this little performance-based guy – and said what?)
> What a good boy am I!

I have a problem with this. He says 'What a good boy am I!' Why is he sitting in the corner? I know why little boys get put in the corner. And in the pictures I saw he had a whole pie on his lap. I've never known of a mother to give a child a whole pie so he must have stolen that from the kitchen. And what's he doing with his fingers in the food, breaking all the social standards of good eating habits? What is he doing taking credit for himself? His mother went out and bought those plums and baked the pie. He should say 'What a great Mom I have!' But performance-based Christians are just like that. When you are a performance-based Christian and you're following all the rules, you think you're really good. It is a really bad day when you forget that you are a deep, deep debtor to the grace of God because you are so fallen. We are so sinful before him. The new covenant comes and liberates us from all of that externalism that deceives us and defiles us with pride.

Listen to Jesus Christ as he speaks to these disciples who are in trauma because he announced that he is leaving. All their dreams have been destroyed. They thought he was going to be the military, social, economic, political conqueror: the Messiah who would overthrow the oppression of Rome, restore Israel to its past glory and guess who was going to sit in the cabinet? They were! They were going to be big shots in the kingdom. Then Jesus announces it's not going to end like that because he's come to give his life for the sins of this world. There they are, locked in trauma and he begins rolling out the comfort of the new covenant.

He will be in you

Jesus Christ said in that Upper Room: 'I will ask the Father, and He will give you another Helper, that He may be with you forever; that is the Spirit of truth, whom the world cannot receive, because it does not see Him or know Him, but you know Him because He abides with you and will be in you' (Jn 14:16-17). The internal dwelling of God within the believer is step one to the internality of the new covenant.

Come to chapter 16 where Jesus reminds them of this again, in verse 7, 'But I tell you the truth, it is to your advantage that I go away; for if I do not go away, the Helper will not come to you: but if I go, I will send Him to you.'

This verse always bothered me a lot. What advantage is it to lose Jesus? But if Jesus did not send the internal Holy Spirit, Jesus being with them would still be external! What would happen when you're in Bethlehem and he's in Jerusalem and you can't speed-dial him on your phone? Here's the advantage – now God would dwell in us, which makes God portable, with us everywhere we go, regardless. He dwells in us, the eternal internal reality of the new covenant.

There's some very profound thought here. God has always wanted to dwell with his people. In the garden of Eden, if I'd walked back into the garden, I'd have wanted to annihilate everybody. But God called them out of the bushes, shed the blood of the animal, clothed them in that early sacrifice for sin: so that there could be a relationship with him again. Then when they went into the wilderness, he would tabernacle with them. Remember all the instructions on how to build the portable tabernacle, so he could go with them and be with them, though veiled, in the Holy of Holies? Then in Jerusalem, when they got into the Promised Land, Solomon built that great temple, fit for the glory of the dwelling God.

God has always wanted to dwell with his people. We get to John chapter 1 where we read that 'we beheld his glory ... the glory as of the only begotten of the Father'. Jesus Christ came and pitched his tent among us. That's literally what the Greek says there. The incarnate God, in Jesus Christ, this tabernacling God, has set up his temple. Where? You are the temple. It's never been like this before. It's why Paul wrote in 1 Corinthians 6:19,20, 'Do you not know that your body is a temple of the Holy Spirit who is in you, whom you have from God, and that you are not your own? For you have been bought with a price: therefore glorify God in your body.'

Is anybody getting how deep and rich this is; that we are a unique people, that he now temples in us? I am his temple. The ramifications of that are huge, aren't they? Your body is where the Almighty eternal God lives. You are the temple: be careful what you put in that temple.

Intimacy

Then he goes on to say in chapter 14:18 'I will not leave you as orphans; I will come to you. After a little while the world will no longer see Me; but you will see Me; because I live, you will live also. In that day you will know that I am in My Father, and you in Me, and I in you' (Jn. 14:18-20). All of a sudden, it's smacking of intimacy, the second aspect of the new covenant. 'He who has My commandments and keeps them is the one who loves Me and he who loves Me will be loved by My Father and I will love him and will disclose Myself to him' (Jn 14:21). This wonderful statement, that the indwelling Spirit personifies Jesus Christ, gives us the capacity of deep intimacy with

Christ. No longer will God be hidden behind the veils of the temple, accessible only by the high priest. Now, in the person of the Holy Spirit, Christ dwells within me and I can intimately fellowship with the living Christ in my heart.

This chapter is book-ended by intimate references. In chapter 13 he tells his disciples he's leaving and they're struck with sorrow. Then in chapter 14:1-3 he says:

> Do not let your heart be troubled; believe in God, believe also in Me. In My Father's house are many dwelling places; if it were not so, I would have told you; for I go to prepare a place for you. If I go and prepare a place for you, I will come again and receive you to Myself, so that where I am, there you may be also.

We don't quite get it but these guys got it because he was talking there about the Jewish marriage scheme. That was a reference to marriage, the ultimate day when we will go home to be with Christ. The church is the bride and he is the bridegroom. What you need to know is that when Jewish people got married, in that day, the suitor, the soon-to-be groom, would strike a covenant deal with the father of the bride and that would be sealed with a glass of wine. Then he would go home to his father's house and he would prepare an apartment in his father's house for the bride. Now the interesting part is that the bride never knew when he was coming back to get her. But when the apartment was finished, one evening he would start through the streets of the village with his best men, torches raised, and they would be shouting in the streets 'The bridegroom cometh!' Isn't this a wonderful picture now of the return of Christ? Then everybody in the village would join the procession with torches yelling 'The bridegroom cometh, the bridegroom cometh!' You can imagine the nervous bride, hoping she would be ready on time. Then he would come and take her and when Jesus said to these disciples 'I go to prepare a place for you. If I go and prepare a place for you, I will come again and receive you to Myself,' you catch the wonderful intimacy that these disciples would have thought about when Christ made that statement.

The rules of intimacy

Chapter 15 is book-ended on the other side by intimacy, that great passage on abiding. Jesus said: 'It is possible for you to abide in me, and I abide in you, like a vine abides with its branches.' Verse 8,

> My Father is glorified by this, that you bear much fruit, and so prove to be My disciples. Just as the Father has loved Me, I have also loved you; abide in My love. If you keep My commandments, you will abide in My love; just as I have kept My Father's commandments and abide in His love.

Do you understand that there are rules to intimacy? I understand that in my relationship with Martie. For us to be soul mates, heart mates, I just can't come home, grab the remote and coast through the TV channels, eat dinner, not say thank you, hit the remote again in my easy chair ... Anybody believe that intimacy's going to happen if I did that all the time? I've got to stop not listening when she talks. I'd like to have a $5 bill for every time she's said to me 'Have you heard anything that I've said?'

There are rules to intimacy, aren't there? Christ, who dwells in you, longs not only for future intimacy when he comes to take you home to heaven but present abiding intimacy now. John writes that the key is obedience. When we surrender to him, when we obey him, we are found with him. If you wonder why intimacy is so elusive for you, could it be that you harbour bitterness in your heart? I want you to know that Jesus doesn't do bitterness. He is the grand forgiver. Unless you obey him, love your enemies, bless those who curse you and pray for those who despitefully use you, you'll keep wondering why he seems so far away.

The Jews complained about a lack of intimacy with God even though they did all the fasts and obeyed all the sacrificial laws and all the feasts. God said, 'Is not this the fast that I have chosen, that you feed the hungry, and you clothe the naked, and you help the oppressed to go free?' If you want to know where Jesus is, often his ministry found him not with the religious folks but with the losers, the lame, the helpless, the hurting, the poor and the oppressed. That's where he is, that's where you find him. This wonderful new covenant privilege of intimacy with the internal dwelling God in the person of the Holy Spirit comes when we get where he is. Martie and I are going to have zero intimacy if I'm never home. Where is Jesus? Where is his heart? Where is his mind? Be there. That's where your hearts will meet; that's where you'll become heart mates with him. That's the joy of the new covenant, that intimacy is a potential possibility for us.

The illuming work of the Holy Spirit

We said last night that the old covenant was instructional; people kept forgetting all of the time and they had to be reinstructed about who God was. So Jesus says, in the Upper Room Discourse in chapter 16:12, 'I have many more things to say to you, but you cannot bear them now. But when He, the Spirit of truth, comes, He will guide you into all the truth.' Remember he is dwelling within you. This is a sense of that writing his laws on your heart; he will help you know God instinctively from the inside out. Keep reading:

> But when He, the Spirit of truth, comes, He will guide you into all the truth; for He will not speak on His own initiative, but whatever He hears, He will speak; and He will disclose to you what is to come. He will glorify Me, for He will take of Mine and will disclose it to you. All things that the Father has are Mine; therefore I said that He takes of Mine and will disclose it to you (Jn.16:13-15).

So this indwelling internal Spirit, who affords you intimacy with Christ as you align yourself with Christ, also is the one that is bringing the truth of Christ to you on the inside. How many of you have ever been reading the Bible and all of a sudden a passage of Scripture just leaps out at you? Anybody ever had that experience? It's the internal instructional work of the Holy Spirit. If you don't believe me, take it to your pagan neighbour, knock on the door and say, 'You are not going to believe this – look at this, this is so wonderful, isn't it, what do you think?' What's the difference? It's the new covenant. The Spirit illumines the word of God for you.

By the way, the internal teaching work of the Holy Spirit, which gives you an intuitive sense about the truth, is always in line with and according to the revealed word of God. The Holy Spirit never does double speak. You're under the teaching of the word of God and all of a sudden something hits you, as the Holy Spirit has been bringing forth the truth to you. Have you ever had a new covenant spark? Every once in a while, someone will come 'Joe, when you said that tonight, it was just what I needed from God.' And you press the rewind button and I didn't say that – I know I never said that! Maybe integrity demands that you say 'I never said that, scratch the blessing!' I don't say that, because I know that dwelling within God's people is the Holy Spirit and the internal teaching work of the Holy Spirit takes the top word and frames it and forms it in a way that you needed to hear it and you've said 'Thank God I've heard from God tonight …' It's that new covenant privilege of the intuitive work, down deep inside of the Holy Spirit.

Martie and I were ministering in Hawaii and someone said, why don't you go on a whale watching boat ride? I'd never seen whales before, so we got on this boat and we go out and here are these humpback whales. This boat stops and all of a sudden they start surfacing around us. And it was magnificent. The naturalist on the boat started telling us about these whales. They grow to be forty feet long, they weigh a ton a foot and when they birth their babies, their babies are born breech. She said 'They have to be born breech or they'd drown in the birthing process. A midwife humpback whale comes and pushes the whale up to the surface so it can take its first baby breath.' I'm going 'Oh my goodness, what a great Creator I have!' How do they know how to birth their whales, their babies, in the shallow waters away from predators?

Then she told us about the song. Every humpback whale in the world sings the same song and next year it'll change by 25 per cent and every humpback whale in the world will sing the new song. In four years from now it'll be a totally different song. I'm going 'Oh God, you are so good, you are the wonderful Creator.' It's a new covenant thing; intuitively, that moment was being ruled by God and the Holy Spirit was taking me to my Creator. That's the wonderful internal work of the Holy Spirit, that he will guide you into all truth.

The Holy Spirit facilitates

Let me read Hebrews chapter 10:15.

> And the Holy Spirit also testifies to us; for after saying, 'This is the covenant that I will make with them after those days,' says the LORD; 'I will put My laws upon their heart, and on their mind I will write them,' He then says, 'And their sins and their lawless deeds I will remember no more.'
>
> Now when there is forgiveness of these things, there is no longer any offering for sin.

That is the new covenant privilege of being declared innocent and all of this we have in Jesus Christ, through the indwelling of the Spirit. It is safe to say there has never been a season of belief in the history of God's work on this planet that has been more privileged than this season of belief, for we are the first wave of people in this wonderful gift, this internal, intimate, intuitive, innocent gift called the new covenant that we participate in. And what's clear is that the Holy Spirit is the facilitator of the new covenant.

There are some ramifications here for us. Since he is the facilitator of the new covenant, and all the privileges of the new covenant are born in us through him, doesn't that say something about our sensitivity to the Holy Spirit? When was the last time you got up in the morning and said 'This morning I will live, starting now, with a deep sensitivity to the presence of the internal, teaching work of the Holy Spirit, to draw me to intimacy with Christ'? When was the last time you woke up and said that? I have to tell you, we like to spend a lot of time talking about all the supernatural manifestations of the Holy Spirit. Come on, take a breath from all of that. What I want to do is drive home to our hearts the urgency of us understanding what is clear about the Holy Spirit in the Bible. And that is that he is the facilitator of the new covenant and if he indwells me as he does that, then

I must be sensitive to him, sensitive to his voice when he speaks to me. In John 10 Jesus said 'My sheep hear my voice and I know them and they follow me.' For us every day of our lives and every situation of our lives, we need to listen for the internal teaching voice of the Spirit that leads us to intimacy with Christ, all day long. If someone comes and confronts you, here's what you need to do: stop and listen to Jesus in the person of the Spirit. Rock back on your heels and just glaze over for a minute. They'll say, 'What are you doing?' 'Checking with the Spirit.' And don't move till you get the signal.

A friend of mine was on a ministry trip. You would probably know his name. He was all alone in a city. He got in the night before his speaking engagement and got to the hotel, checked in, got on the elevator and these two gorgeous young women were on the elevator. He pressed the button and he said 'What floor do you want?' They said, 'We're going to any floor you're going to. How about a little fun tonight? Who would know?' He said, in that moment, it was like a sheet came down with Galatians written on it 'He who sows to the flesh shall reap the corruption of the flesh.' That was a new covenant moment where the Spirit of God was speaking to him.

I'm an incurable people person, but people people get peopled out sometimes and at the end of a long people day in ministry, I would get in the car and I would be alone. I would say 'I'm going home, I'm going to head for the big closet and tell Martie to slide supper and the newspaper under the door. Don't talk to me for three hours. That's what I'm going to do.' Then the Holy Spirit would start working; it's a new covenant moment. He'd say 'Joe, who's at home?' I'd say 'People.' And then he'd take me to Ephesians 5, 'Husbands, love your wives as Christ loved the church.' And to Ephesians 6: you know – don't irritate your children and discourage them and lead them to anger by disappointing them and not loving and caring for them. 'You mean, Lord, I've got to go home and talk to Martie about her day and wrestle with the kids on the floor?' 'Got it.' That was the Spirit. Do any of you ever experience that?

That leads me to step two of the facilitating work of the Spirit. Paul says, 'Quench not the Spirit of God within you.' You want to tank this whole new covenant stuff? Quenching the Spirit is telling him 'Shh,

I don't want to hear that right now. I'm not ready for that.' And do not grieve the Spirit of God, which is going against his voice, sinning intentionally, telling him 'I know you told me that but I will do this, thank you.' It's not just listening, it's refusing to quench, it's refusing to grieve this Holy Spirit of the new covenant who dwells within us. Then it's Galatians 5 – walk in the Spirit. Stay in this fear of the Spirit; don't ever get out of his Spirit. All your walking, whatever you do, stay within this fear of the Spirit; if it's in the Spirit, it's cool: if it's not, it's out of bounds. Then Paul tells us that those who walk in the Spirit and by the Spirit, you can tell they're walking there because their lives are characterised by character; love, joy, peacemakers, patient people, kind people, good people, people of self-control. You can tell a new covenant person a mile away by the character of Christ that emanates from their lives. It's one thing to rejoice in the new covenant, it's quite another thing to get on board with the facilitator of the new covenant, this indwelling Holy Spirit, and let him unfold all the privileges of the new covenant for you.

Living water

The Jews had a interesting practice. The feast of the tabernacles was a seven-day feast in Jerusalem and they had gala events all the time. This feast celebrated their wandering in the wilderness and they set up little huts all over the city as though they were still dwelling in tents and tabernacles. The leading ritual of the feast was that every day the high priest, decked in his robes and accompanied by a levitical chorus and trumpets, would go down to the pool of Siloam, bring a large basin of water back, march around the altar once and pour the water out. The water would go gushing down the stairs as a reminder that it was the God of Israel who prospered them with water in the dry and thirsty land.

But on the seventh day, on the last great day of the festival, there were seven priests in a gala procession, and twenty-one trumpets of the levitical trumpet squad. The levitical chorus and all of the people marched down to the pool of Siloam praising God, as seven huge large buckets of water were drawn from the pool of Siloam and a choir sang. They would go back up to the temple and these priests carrying these large vials of water would walk seven times around the altar, while the people shouted 'Save us, O Lord! Please Lord save us, save us, O Lord! Please, Lord!' The joy and the crying out was huge and, as the trumpets blared and the levitical choruses sang on the seventh time around the altar, the priest took that water, poured it on the altar and the gushing flow of that water would roll down the steps to the feet of the shouting people: 'Please Lord save us, O God our Lord, save us!'

John tells us that it was in that moment, on the last day of the great day of the feast, that Jesus stood and shouted out as the waters came down. 'If any man is thirsty, let him come to Me and drink. He who believes in me, from his innermost being shall flow rivers of water.' Then John adds 'But this He spoke of the Spirit whom those who believed in him were to receive. For the Spirit was not yet given because Jesus was not yet glorified.'

This is the glory of the gospel.

Born identity (1)

Introduction

It's a bad thing to be lost, isn't it? Today Martie and I were driving down the back country road to Buttermere and all of a sudden, I don't know where I am! It will be a great encouragement to all you women to know that today there was a man in England who reached for a map! So I reached back for the map to find out, where am I?

I think one of the great challenges that we have in our walk with Christ is that we really don't know where we are and this leads me to our text, 2 Corinthians 5:17. Paul writes to the church at Corinth, 'Therefore, if anyone is in Christ, he is a new creation.'

'Therefore if any man is in Christ': in Christ, that's where you are. I have to admit that hanging out in the church world all of my life, I've got just a little frustrated with the fact that we've got all these church words that we throw around. We all know them, like we are 'in Christ', we know all the words but we rarely drill down and understand what it means. To be in Christ means to have access to and participation in all that he is and all that he offers to you.

Now we can understand it like this. I have access to my pocket; I have a right to what's in my pocket. If you go in there, you're nicking what's in my pocket. You don't have a right to do that. I wonder what's in here? Access to what? Here's two £20 notes! Fish and chips afterwards tonight. What else do I have access to in here? A hotel room key, a place to sleep tonight. What else ... car keys. I don't have to walk home on Friday. And a house key! That's so I can get in when I get home. And Master Card! Whatever I want that pleases my wicked little heart ... and a cash card. Do you realise I can stick this in a bank in Keswick's cash machine, put my pin number in, and within forty seconds get money out of my bank account in Chicago at the exact exchange rate in pounds? I'm happy this is in my pocket. Are you getting the picture, by the way?

I have an identity in Christ, as you do; because in him, if you are in him, you are a new creation. All that silliness just to anchor in your brain that if you are in Christ you have access to and participation in all that he offers you and all that he is. It's huge.

Who gets the privilege?

In Galatians chapter 3:27, Paul makes it very clear. 'For all of you who were baptised into Christ ...' We'll stop here. He's not talking about water baptism, he's talking about Holy Spirit baptism, that act of the Holy Spirit when, at the point of your conversion, in coming to Christ, he immerses you into the person of Jesus Christ. Who gets the privilege? Every single person, who has been to the bloodstained cross and embraced the offer of salvation, is put into Christ at the moment of salvation.

'And have clothed yourself' – this is a beautiful picture, that you and I actually are clothed with Jesus Christ. What strikes me is what comes next: 'And if you belong to Christ, then you are Abraham's descendants, heirs according to promise.' In another part of the text (verse 28) he writes that this is true of everybody, whether slave or free, male or female, regardless of who you are. I love that. A lot of us, most of us, are just flat out nobodies. We don't count, nobody knows our names, we think we're not much at all. Wake up to this wonderful truth: you are in Christ, regardless of who you are. Jesus Christ is an equal person-welcomer. Get your chin up, get a sense of deep satisfaction that you in Christ and have access and participation in all that he is, regardless of who you are.

As Martie and I were driving, we stopped at this pub and sat out in the garden and had a wonderful lunch. As we were finishing our lunch, a couple came up and they happened to be from Keswick. They introduced themselves and they had two little kids and we chatted for a while. Then their little girl looks at me and says, 'Excuse me. Were you saved when you were six?' Remember I mentioned that the other night? I said, 'Yeah, I was.' She said, 'So was I.' I said, 'Isn't that wonderful?' She said, 'Yes, on Boxing Day.' She started giving me her testimony. She said, 'And Jesus has meant so much to me. I try to stick up for him with my friends and when my friends use his name in vain, I tell them they shouldn't do that. Some of them do it anyway but I've got a real good friend who said, "Well, if you don't like it, I won't do it either." And Jesus has been good to me through some hard times. I haven't had many hard times and they weren't real long but I don't know what people would do if they didn't have Jesus.' I said, 'How old are you?' She said, 'I'm ten.' You see, it doesn't make any difference. This ten-year-old girl, Bethany, is in Christ, with access to and participation in all that Jesus offers. That's who gets it. You are in Christ.

What is it worth?

In Philippians chapter 3, Paul lists all his credentials and gives all the things that he could brag about and it's really pretty spectacular if you're Jewish. Then he shocks us in verse 7. He says:

> But whatever things were gain to me, those things I have counted as loss for the sake of Christ. More than that, I count all things to be loss in view of the surpassing value of knowing Christ Jesus my Lord, for whom I have suffered the loss of all things, and count them but rubbish so that I may gain Christ, and may be found in Him, not having a righteousness of my own derived from the Law, but that which is through faith in Christ, the righteousness which comes from God on the basis of faith (Phil. 3:7-9).

I'm here to tell you, it is worth everything … Paul said, 'I count the best most valuable things in my life to be like rubbish compared to the surpassing value of being found in Christ.' He knew what great value this was and what great worth this brings.

What would this mean in your life?

We noticed in Galatians that when we are in Christ, we are clothed in him. Paul says that when he is in Christ he is wrapped in the righteousness of Christ. And we read in Revelation that we are clothed in the white robes of God's righteousness and this unlocks for us some very profound meanings.

Confident prayer life

Suddenly you feel a press in your heart and the need to pray, so you're running into the throne room of God. If you went in there by yourself, you'd be fried, in a moment, by the terror of his appropriate wrath against your sin. You would have brought yourself into his holy presence that cannot be defiled by sin and it would have been the right thing for him to consume you in your sin. We don't stand a chance in prayer if we do not approach the throne wrapped in the righteousness of Jesus Christ. Turn to Hebrews chapter 4, which tells us about the confidence we can have in effective prayer, being in Christ. The writer to Hebrews writes 'Therefore, since we have a great high priest who has passed through the heavens, Jesus the Son of God, let us hold fast our confession ... (Heb. 4:14)' If you are in Christ and Jesus has passed through the heavens into the throne room, you are in Christ in the presence of the Almighty God, in the throne room before God.

Jesus the high priest

One of the themes of the book of Hebrews is the priesthood of Christ. In the day that this was written, the high priest was not someone the people could identify with. The position of high priest was political, bought and sold in the bureaucracies of Rome: someone who lived far above the fray of normal life, someone who could not identify with the people in any respect. He went once a year into the holy of holies to represent the people but they would have felt 'He's clueless about what I struggle with. He can't represent me.' So out of that common thought pattern, the writer to Hebrews writes this:

> Since we have a great high priest who has passed through the heavens, Jesus the Son of God, let us hold fast our confession. For we do not have a high priest who cannot sympathize with our weaknesses, but One who has been tempted in all things as we are, yet without sin. Therefore let us draw near with confidence ... (Heb. 4:14-16).

The Greek word there is boldness, literally unstaggering confidence: 'Therefore let us draw near with confidence to the throne of grace, so that we may receive mercy and find grace to help in time of need' (Heb. 4:16).

When you go in prayer, you go in Christ. You walk into the throne room and God says to Jesus, 'Who's that?' Jesus says, 'It's all right, he's with me. It's OK. She's with me. It's all right, he's in me, she's in me.' And we can pour out our hearts in prayer in confidence because we are in Christ, our great high priest, tested in all ways as we are.

Effective prayer

One of the highlight memories of my life in ministry happened two years ago here at Keswick. It was Sunday morning, they asked me to speak in a local church here, the Crosthwaite church, just out at the edge of town. I'd never been to that church but the singing was wonderful and the pastor said, 'I've asked sister so-and-so to come and do the church prayers and after that I've asked her to share a word about what the Keswick week means to her.'

So she prayed and then said, 'During a Keswick week several years ago, I was working in a bakery down in the town and a lady from the conference came in every single day. Her name was Winnie. She struck up a friendship with me. There was something different about her, and when the week was gone I was so sorry to see her go. I looked for her the next year and I didn't see her but I couldn't get Winnie off my mind.' Then the lady said 'One day I began to feel a drawing of my heart to Jesus Christ. It was so compelling it was almost physical. I tried to forget it, I tried to put it away, but every day this drawing of my heart to Jesus Christ was there. I was walking by the church and walked in and saw the pastor' and she told the pastor and the pastor led her to the Lord.

The next year the Keswick week came and she's looking for Winnie. And someone walks in and says, 'By the way, do you remember a lady by the name of Winnie? She's not here but she wanted to say "Hi!" to you.' And the lady said 'Please tell Winnie that I've accepted Christ as my Saviour.' And the other lady said 'Winnie has prayed for you every single day since she left Keswick.'

I want to ask you a question. If Winnie hadn't been in Christ, could those prayers have soared through the territory of Satan? Could she have approached the throne if she had not been in Christ, if Christ hadn't been working? No! A thousand times no. It was Winnie in Christ that made those prayers work.

That's a long story but I had to tell it to you to encourage you that, if you are in Christ, you can have confidence in effective prayer. Stay at it, don't give up. You are being represented at the throne by Jesus Christ. You are accessing and participating in all that he offers you because you are in Christ.

Victory over sin

Some of our prayers will be about our struggle with sin. Being in Christ means that you have, guaranteed in him, victory over sin. The cross, if I can explain this clearly, was Satan's finest hour. Satan had done what he'd tried to do through the whole Old Testament: defeated the Messiah's seed and defeated the promise of that coming victory over Satan and hell forever in the person of the Messiah. Satan had won, the Messiah was dead on the tree, and for three days in hell Beelzebub oversaw a party of celebration. Then on the third day, with Beelzebub on his throne in victory, someone whispers a bad piece of news in his ear. 'He's risen.' 'No, that can't be! We put soldiers at the grave!' 'Yes he's risen, he's alive.' In that moment, Jesus Christ struck the death knell blow to Satan and to sin and to death. He is the Victor; we read that in 1 Corinthians chapter 15, in that great resurrection chapter where Paul is explaining all the significance of the resurrection and then he says 'The sting of death is sin and the strength of sin is the law but thanks be to God, who gives us the victory through the Lord Jesus Christ' (I Cor. 15:56-57).

It reminded me of a story I heard about a custodian who worked in a seminary and during his lunch hour he had his Bible on his lap. An erudite seminary professor walked by and said, 'I'm sure you don't understand that.' And the custodian said, 'Oh, I do.' The professor goes 'Really? What does it mean?' The custodian says, 'It means Jesus wins.'

It means Jesus wins; the conqueror. If you are in Christ you don't need to fail. You may want to fail, you might fail, but you don't need to fail. I need not fear sin, I need not fear my adversary, no matter what I'm up against, I am in the Victor, the person of Jesus Christ, and in Jesus Christ, you have victory over sin if you are in Christ. Do you know how important it is to know where you are?

Sheltered in his protection

If you are in Christ, you are sheltered in his protection. How many of you know that you are in Satan's cross-hairs? I want us to all wake up to the fact we are at war. All right? This is not Eden any more and while you have victory over sin, because you are in Jesus Christ, there will be times when you will feel vulnerable and open to the onslaught of Satan in your life. I want you to know that you are sheltered in his protective care because you are in him. It simply means this: Satan can't get to you without going through Jesus Christ. You say, 'How come I have this stuff in my life, then?' Because Jesus has permitted it to come into your life.

Look at Job, for instance. Satan came to God and God said to him, 'Where have you been?' He said, 'Walking to and fro across the face of this earth.' God said, 'Have you seen my man Job?' Do you know what? I just pray that God could say that about me. And Satan said 'Yeah, I saw him' and Satan then accuses God, in front of all the angelic hosts, by saying, 'The only reason Job is so righteous and good is you buy him off! You have been good to him and that is why!'

It was God's character that was at stake. Is God worthy to be worshipped and praised, regardless of what is happening in your life?

Absolutely he is. Satan is saying 'You are not worthy to be praised regardless of what is happening. You have to buy people's favour. You have to pay them off to get them to worship.' He had slandered the name of God. Job did not suffer for any earthly reason at all. He suffered for God's reputation in the universe. God said, 'OK. You can get him, but only this far' (Job 1).

Remember the restrictions that God put? God said, 'We're going to prove a point here. Job's going to be my man.' To prove that God is worthy to be worshipped and praised regardless of what happens in a person's life, in spite of his lame wife who said, 'Curse God and die!', God permitted Satan to move in for a purpose. Always remember that. Here's the protective work of God. It's proof positive that Satan has to go through Jesus to get to you. If Jesus lets him through, it is for a purpose. Even the thorn in the flesh of Paul, that was for a purpose, so that he would not be proud. Pride ruins a ministry. It was so that he could be humbled and know in his weakness that God would be strong.

Joseph was sold in that brutal betrayal by his brothers, this righteous young man. 'God, why did you let that happen?' He gets sold into Egypt. He withstands seduction in a season of life when his hormones ran hot and God said, 'Ha, my kind of man! Three years in a slammer!' The purpose was to refine his arrogance and to humble his heart, so God could use him to rise to power and save the Messiah's seed from starvation. When his brothers came and trembled, he pronounced this wonderful age-old verdict. Joseph said, 'You meant it for evil but God meant it for good' (Gen. 50:20). If you are in Christ, all things work together for good. Jesus is in charge of moving all of history to eternity, where Satan will realise his final eternal defeat and Eden will be restored with no possibility of failure. You are in him. Is that significant? You say, 'I'm not important.' You are: the big plan has bits and pieces and you are part of the bits and pieces in your world where you live. If you are in Christ, you are a part of that plan and anything he lets in is planned with purpose. God never wastes your sorrows because you are in Christ.

Can I read a passage of Scripture to you?

What then shall we say to these things? If God is for us, who is against us? He who did not spare His own Son, but delivered Him over for us all, how will He not also with Him freely give us all things? Who will bring a charge against God's elect? God is the one who justifies; who is the one who condemns? Christ Jesus is He who died, yes, rather who was raised, who is at the right hand of God, who also intercedes for us.

Who will separate us from the love of Christ? Will tribulation, or distress, or persecution, or famine, or nakedness, or peril, or sword?

Just as it is written, 'For your sake we are being put to death all day long; we were considered sheep to be slaughtered.' But in all these things we overwhelmingly conquer through Him who loved us. For I am convinced that neither death, nor life, nor angels, nor principalities, nor things present, nor things to come, nor powers, nor height, nor depth, nor any other created thing, will be able to separate us from the love of God, which is in Christ Jesus our Lord.

Where is this love found? 'In Christ Jesus.' So the fact that you are in him guarantees that you are sheltered and protected and that everything in your life has purpose and that there is a plan and that there is progress in it, and you can count on that.

Trust

I slipped into a little Baptist church in Chipping Camden, Gloucestershire, one Sunday morning. And in the course of the service the pastor said, 'I've asked sister so-and-so to come and do the church prayers.' And as she began to pray about the things of the church, she said, 'Lord, we do not know why it is that you have seen fit to take another child from our church, and I pray for Peter' and I forget the wife's name 'who have lost their little baby this week. Nor, Lord, do we understand why in this year you have taken three of our babies home.' Then she broke down and she couldn't continue. But then she regained her strength and I'll never forget what she said. She said, 'Lord, it is not ours to ask why but only to trust you, so teach us to trust you.' That was an 'in Christ' prayer; to trust him when you don't understand what's happening, to trust that in Christ there is purpose, that he doesn't waste our sorrows.

Or should we talk about his wisdom? To be in Christ, you have access to his wisdom. How many times in my life I've just flown off [the handle.] In James chapter 1 we read that if you ask God for his wisdom, he says, 'You can have access to that.' I remember one day having one of those insoluble problems. I didn't know what to do. It was big and I was clueless. I knew that what I thought I ought to do was probably outside the pale of his pleasure. I had a forty-minute drive from a hospital back to my office and I turned off the radio and said, I've got to be quiet, and I just pleaded with God, 'Could you help me to know what to do?' And it was a new covenant moment, as he was bringing Scripture passages back to me. Forty minutes later, I pulled into my parking place and I knew just what to do, because of the access that I had to the wisdom of Christ by being in Christ.

Heaven

Where would you be when life's clock stops ticking? Where would you be on the precipice of eternity if you weren't in Christ? I have a pastor friend who travels in troubled Third World countries, where he's often hassled at the border and in one sermon I was listening to him preach, he said 'I get hassled at a lot of borders but with Jesus on my passport I won't be hassled at the border of heaven!' Is there anybody here that's glad that this isn't the only world we have? This is the short nasty brutish one, this is the fallen one: would we please stop expecting to find all of our happiness, joy, comfort and satisfaction here? It's not going to happen. This is the fallen world, this is the domain of the enemy, this is warfare time. But that glad day is coming when Jesus will call us home, and we'd walk by the gate, and there would be Peter. And he takes one look at you and one look at Jesus and Jesus says 'It's all right, he's with me.' You're in because you are in Christ. You are in Christ, with access to and participation in all that he offers and all that he is. Could there be a better gift of the new covenant – a better gift of grace? For all of you who have thinking about Jesus in you, that's a pretty important thought; maybe you ought to start about thinking a little bit about that you are in Jesus and all that that means.

There is a man who is a collector of great art; a multi-millionaire. He and his wife travelled all over the world collecting great art. Their house was full of masterpieces, but then his wife died. He was broken hearted. She was his soul mate. But he had a son and his son and he were deeply bonded and then his son was called to go to war and the horrible day came when he received notification that his son had been killed in battle. And he was all alone. The art didn't mean anything to him any more, and he became a hermit, lived inside this mansion.

One day there was a knock at a door and there was this dishevelled guy with half a leg and a crutch and a package under his arm. He said, 'Sir' and he named the son's name, 'are you his dad?' and he said, 'Yes.' He said, 'I have something I thought I'd give to you. I was in the war with your son and he and I were best friends and I'm an artist, so one day I drew a picture of your son. I know that he got killed and I thought maybe you'd like the picture?' So the man reached out and unwrapped it and it's crude; it wasn't worth anything but it was a picture of his son. He took it in and took down the greatest masterpiece of all and hung his son's picture there.

Then the day came when the guy died. All the world was clamouring for a shot at his collection, and Sothebys was the auction house of choice. On the day that it was all to be auctioned, art collectors from all over the world gathered. You can imagine the excitement in that auction house when the auctioneer called the auction open. And as he did this, the war veteran who had painted the picture of the son slipped in the back row, unnoticed. The auctioneer took the veil off the first masterpiece on the easel and it was the picture of the son. And the auctioneer said, 'Do I hear fifty dollars? Will anybody give me fifty dollars? Forty, thirty, twenty, fifteen?' The place was silent. Finally, the wounded soldier at the back said, 'I'll give you fifteen.' He says, 'Going once, going twice; to the man in the back. The auction is closed.' And everyone was murmuring, saying, 'What about everything else?' The auctioneer took out the man's will and said, 'It is in the man's will that whoever takes the son gets it all.' If you take the Son, you get it all and that's the glory of the gospel.

Born identity (2)

Introduction

If you were to ask me what my favourite movies have been in the last three years, on my short list would be the movie *Bourne Identity*. It's a great movie. Matt Damon, the lead character through most of it, is lost in a horrible case of total amnesia. He has no idea who he is. At one point in the movie, he and his girlfriend are lost and she says, 'Where are we?' In frustration, he says, 'Don't ask me that question. I don't even know who I am!' That's a terrible place to be, isn't it?

I've come all the way from Chicago to give you a piece of good news – when you came to Jesus Christ, you received a born identity. When you were born again, God gave you a very special identity. What I sense is a problem with God's people is that we are often lost in this horrible case of spiritual amnesia, not knowing who we are. And if you don't know who you are, your life is probably not going to be as God wants it to be. Your sense of identity tends to shape your behaviour: I learned that when I was a kid. My dad's a preacher and so they affectionately called me a PK – preacher's kid. I'd like to have a £5 note for every time people in the church said to me, 'You're the pastor's son' (identity) 'you should be an example.' I didn't want to be an example; I was only five! I wanted to have fun with my friends but all of that was so that I would live up to my identity.

I wonder if you know what your identity is in Jesus Christ. If I were to see you and say, 'How are you?' and you really had a grip on this, you'd say, 'Thank you for asking. I am an NCPer.' We are people who are in Christ. 2 Corinthians 5:17, 'Therefore, if any of us is in Christ, he is a new creation.' That's where NCPer comes from: a new creation person. What does that mean? What are its ramifications for our lives?

The old creation order

In order to understand that we are new creation people, we have to realise that if there's a new creation, there was an old creation. In order to have new creation there had to be an old creation. I want to paint the old creation and its dynamics as a backdrop against what Paul is teaching us here. According to the New Testament, Jesus Christ is the Creator but in Genesis 1, it is the Holy Spirit doing the work of creation. Christ is the Creator and the Holy Spirit is the executive director of creation. We read that darkness, a great void, was over all of what would become the universe; and we read that the Holy Spirit hovered – the Hebrew word is like a bird hovering – over the creation. He spoke to the nothingness and day and night were born. The seas became and then were parted and dry land appeared. Then on the dry land, birds, flowers appeared and as the creation emerged, the pinnacle point of this old creation was where he picked up the dust of the ground and he blew the breath of life into the dust of the ground and Adam became the pinnacle of creation.

What I love about the creation story is after every single point of creation it says 'and God saw what he had done and it was good'. If God says it's good, it's good. But when he created Adam, he said, 'It is not good that man should be alone.' All of God's women said, 'Amen!'

I wish I had a little time capsule to go back to different places in biblical history. I'd love to be here at this moment when God puts a divine anaesthetic over Adam. Adam falls asleep and then God, out of Adam's side, creates woman. I'd like to be there to watch Adam wake up. Can you imagine the moment? Grogging himself from the anaesthetic, looking around the garden and … whoa! You have to remember this is pre-fall, it is perfection. There was this picture. It was called Eden and it was aesthetically stunning, it was the best that God could do.

Some of you are gardeners. How many of you have really good gardens and you're so proud of how your gardens look? I want you to know as good as your garden gets, it is a garden in a fallen world. Think of what this garden must have been like and the beauty, the aromas of it. There are Adam and Eve, in perfect harmony, in perfect fellowship with their God, finding a depth of satisfaction like you and I have never even imagined.

The fall

Satan said, 'We'll have none of this, thank you.' For Satan is against everything that is beautiful and good and of God. It became his intention to destroy it. Satan, in league with one man, graffitied the face of this beautiful creation and it all fell. God says to Adam, 'What have you done?' And he says, 'It's the woman you gave me.' She blames the serpent and then they're ashamed. Soon emerging in their family is murder and by the end of chapter 4 you have a whole culture that is dominated by a depth of immorality and anarchy. Satan has accomplished his will and taken what has been good and glorious of God and it is damaged beyond repair.

We have tasted the pain of what it means to live in a fallen place, among a fallen race. We bring the baggage in: the baggage of abuse, broken promises, destroyed relationships, fallen choices that we have made that have filled our lives with phenomenal regret. We know the consequence of what happened back in the early part of Scripture where Satan came in and yielded for us a fallen place and a fallen race. What was wonderfully good became horribly bad. And so we say to God, 'Why don't you fix it?' How many of you think God could fix it? How big is your God? But when something is broken, no matter how you fix it, it is never the same again. God did not want to fix this place – he wanted to start all over again. My mind races to Luke chapter 1, where the angel comes to Mary and he says, 'From your womb will be born the promise of the Messiah.' Mary asks the question you would ask, 'But how can this be since I have never known a man?' And the angel says, 'This is how it will be. The Spirit of God will over-shadow you.' This is the Spirit of God starting all over again with a whole new creation in the dark of a woman's womb, to create within that womb something that has never been created before, a God-man who would emerge as the beginning of the new creation. As one man in league with Satan brought terrible defeat, one God-man in league with God would bring about a whole new order, an order that would never fail. When Jesus was born, this new creation, this God-man, came forth as the personification of the new creation, as the leader of new creation, as the facilitator of the new creation. That's who Jesus is; the starting point with God starting all over again.

Now pour that truth back into what Paul is teaching us. Jesus Christ is the new creation: if anyone is in Christ, then the fact that you are in Christ means that you are part and parcel of that new creation. That's why you are an NCPer. That is your fundamental identity. God chose by adoption to place you into the privileged place of the new creation.

Old things are passed away

What would it mean to realise that, in Christ, I'm a privileged part-ner in this whole new order that is emerging through Jesus Christ? Number one, it means that I recognise the ultimate doom of the old order, of the old creation and reject it. Notice what the text says. 'If any man is in Christ, he is a new creation.' Then he does this little phrase 'old things are passed away'. Did you ever scratch your head and say, 'I wonder what those old things are?' In the context of this holy emerging new order, new creation, it is very clear that the old things are the old order – the old system, the lying, the deceit, the murder and the terrorism on London streets and in New York City. It is the old order under the direction of our adversary, Satan.

What is important to note in this text is that when he says 'the old is passed away' the Greek tense is the aorist, which means a past com-pleted action. At some point in history the old order was doomed, in an historical act on this planet. What was that historic act that doomed the old system of Satan? It was the cross; that's where hell and death were defeated; where Satan was damned for eternity. The nails in the hands of Jesus were the nails driven in the coffin of this old order. We need to understand the very nature of this old order, now that it is a doomed, damned, finished order.

But how come it is still going? How come I still feel its impact? I don't know. It's for reasons best known to God in his eternal timelines. What you need to know is the text teaches us that it is doomed and it is done and it is completed. It reminds me of the story of a lorry driver who'd been driving for about twenty years and decides to change companies. But in changing companies he had to have an interview. The interviewer asked him this question: 'If you were driving down this huge hill, and on one side of the hill is a cliff and on the other side another cliff and your brakes and your handbrakes went, what would you do?' He said, 'I'd wake up Nigel.' 'Who's Nigel?' 'Nigel's my driving buddy. We've been driving together for twenty years.' 'Why would you wake up Nigel?' 'We've seen a lot of dramatic accidents and I want to wake up Nigel because he's never seen an accident like we're going to have when we get down the bottom of that hill!'

I want you to know that this old world order is careening downhill, no brakes, ultimately headed for doom and destruction and that is sure because at the cross that was accomplished. NCPers recognise the ultimate doom of this world system. But why is it that you, as an NCPer, still live according to the instincts of this doomed old world order? Why is it that envy grips your heart? Why is it that you manipulate relationships? Why is it that in the darkness of your home, late at night, you're on the computer flirting with the old order? Why is it that people could walk into our churches and not seen anything of the new order? They belong to clubs that probably do better than our churches. I say this to our shame. What could there be in your heart and life that would be vestiges of the damned old order; twinges of greed, seeds of bitterness, that prideful elevation of your nothingness?

The new world order

When Paul writes this, he puts 'all things are becoming new' in the perfect tense. The perfect tense is a past action with continuing results.

If you throw a rock in a pond, you have a big splash and then the waves go out from there. There is a past action with the birth of Jesus Christ, the emerging reality of Jesus, still within the context of the declining world in which we live, racing to its doom. The new creation emerges in a lot of stages. Notice the sequential movement of this. Jesus taught like no man had ever taught before and he brought principles that contradicted the old system. And then he called to himself a new people: you and me, called out of this old order, a new people for himself.

A new freedom

Then he brought about on the cross a new freedom, and then ultimately a whole new day, when he will wipe away every tear and there will be no more sorrow, no more dying and no more death. Can you imagine that? Jesus Christ brings about that new day. And he creates a new heaven and a new earth, Eden again, with no possibility of failure forever.

A new culture

That's what the new creation is all about; it's our privileged participation to embrace the emerging new culture of Christ. This new creation is a dramatically different culture than the world in which we live. I like the way Paul puts it in Colossians chapter 1:13, that when you were redeemed, God transplanted you out of the domain of darkness, into the kingdom of his dear Son. That's a new creation privilege and throughout all of the New Testament this new world order of the new creation is spoken of as the kingdom of Christ. The kingdom of Christ is dramatically different from this world in which we live and as the French say, 'Vive la difference!' This new creation is the kingdom of Jesus Christ!

I went on a missionary trip to Africa, down into that interesting part of West Africa where the sub-Sahara meets the jungle. I couldn't believe how different that culture was. For instance, the larger women are over there, the more beautiful they are considered to be. They have a proverb there that says if you put your wife on a camel and the camel can't stand up, or breaks its legs in the process, you have a

beautiful wife. Women buy it. Husbands force feed their women lard
– this is all true – so that they might become large, because it means
that the husband must be very wealthy and successful if he can feed
his wife that much food. It was so different. I never felt at home there.
I wonder how many of you feel at home in the old doomed order?
Or have you tasted the wonders of the new creation of Jesus Christ?
Do you say, 'I could never feel at home in the old order again because
I'm an NCPer, thanks to Christ.'

New lives

The kingdom of Jesus Christ is a culture that has a constitution. Do
any of you know what the constitution of the new created order is?
It is the Sermon on the Mount. We live dramatically different lives
because we are part of the new created order in Jesus Christ. Christ
does this 'but it shall not be so among you' thing. Do you remember
that in the Gospels? That's a flag to show this is 'old order, new order'
teaching. We don't have time to go through the Sermon on the
Mount but you get to chapter 5 and Jesus Christ says, 'You have heard
it said unto you that you should love your friends and hate your enemies.' That was a proverb of the day. In America, we say 'I don't get
mad, I get even.' You say that here too, don't you? And then he says
'But it shall not be so among you.' Ding! New order moment. He says
'Love your enemies. Bless those who curse you. Pray for those who
despitefully use you.' Where are you on this new order plank in the
constitution of the new created order? Because it's easy to stay in the
old order on that one. I hear you say, 'You do not know what that person did to me.' You're right, I don't. And you say, 'They don't deserve
it!' I agree with you, they don't. You say, 'If I forgive them, that won't
be fair.' By the way, is anybody glad that God wasn't fair with you?

Jesus says, 'Love your enemies, bless those who curse you, pray for
those who despitefully use you, so that you might be like your Father
who is in heaven' – the architect of the new created world order that
is eternal, who has forgiven you. Don't you know that God makes the
sun to shine on bad people? So be like your Father who is in heaven.
How do you get over that hump? Because you're right, they don't
deserve it. You're not doing it for them. Why do I forgive my enemies?

Because I'm an NCPer; I do it for Jesus. I'm a part of the new created order, it has nothing to do with them.

How many times do we have to do this? Seven times? Jesus upped the ante: 'Four hundred and ninety times per offence, OK? And who's counting?' But what strikes me is the story that Jesus told about man who owed literally millions and millions of pounds and was dragged in by the man he owed it to, who demanded he pay it (Mt. 18:23-25). He pleaded 'Have mercy!' And surprisingly the one who held the debt forgave all the debt. Shocking! And the man goes out into the street and finds somebody who owes him just a tiny bit and demands that he pays. That man begs his mercy and he says, 'Absolutely not. I'll have you thrown in the debtors' prison.' Then somebody told the first master about him. And the first master dragged him in and threw him in prison and tormented him because, having been forgiven so much, he refused to give even something small to someone. Jesus said that is how God feels toward us when he has forgiven us such a huge penalty of sin and we refuse to forgive a smaller offence. Every offence is smaller than my offence against God.

New ways of leading

NCPers live dramatically different lives – because they are a part of a dramatically different culture. You're a part of the kingdom of Jesus Christ. Another one of those – 'You have heard it said but I say to unto you' transitions is in Matthew chapter 20 – one of my favourite moments in the Bible. James and John come to make a request of Jesus and they bring their mother along. She says, 'Grant that one of these two sons of mine may sit at your right and the other at your left in your kingdom.' What she was asking for were the positions of power and influence. Anyone who sits to the right or the left of a monarch is a person of power in the kingdom. So when the others heard it, 'they were moved with indignation'. Why were they so upset? Because they all wanted it! These are probably twelve minus one of the most committed, dedicated people that this world has ever known for Jesus Christ. And yet within them is this desire for power, recognition and affirmation. I don't know how committed you are but watch out. There still may be trash within your soul. Jesus says, 'You know that the rulers of the Gentiles lord it over them' – 'that's an old order thing you guys are up to right now.' 'Not so with you. Instead, whoever wants to become great among you must be your servant, and whoever wants to be first must be your slave.' And then he said, speaking of himself, the emerging personification of the new creation, 'just as the Son of Man did not come to be served, but to serve, and to give his life as a ransom for many.'

The mark of the new created order is not only the banner of forgiveness, it is the banner of servanthood. I've studied a lot of theology and you grow accustomed to the stuff you've been around a long time. But I will never grow accustomed to this: that when Jesus Christ came, the emergent leader of this new creation, who could have chosen to sit on the throne in Jerusalem bedecked in expensive robes, demanding that everybody pay homage – he would have been right to do that because he is God – he chose instead the identity of a servant. You say, 'You don't understand, I have a position. I'm a pastor.' Go to Philippians 2 where this emergent new concept in the new order is exemplified in Christ. He used the platform of his power to serve the needs of other people.

I don't always do this well but I've been studying this text. When I was serving Christ at Moody, we had a downtown campus right in the heart of Chicago, so a lot of our buildings are vertical and my office is on the ninth floor. I got on the elevator one day and the inside of the elevator doors are stainless steel and there was a housekeeper in there with a little rag, getting the fingerprints off the doors. She was only about 4 foot 4 inches, so she had this 18 inch shortfall that she couldn't reach, up at the top. I'm watching her, and I'm thinking it's a pity that some common employee didn't get on – they could help her! But not me. I'm the president. The president of places doesn't do that kind of thing ... but right away the Spirit of God has got me in a full nelson against the elevator walls. 'Stowell, are you going to be an NCPer right now? Are you going to be a part of this emerging new world order? Are you going to express servanthood?' I said to her, 'Excuse me, can I help you get that to the top?' and she handed me the rag and the door opened. I just kept doing it. I was on the elevator a couple of months later and I saw her again and asked, 'How are the elevators coming?' She says, 'Great, everybody is helping me with the elevators now!' Be an NCPer: it might catch on! Are you getting the point? If you are in Christ that's where you are; your identity is an NCPer and you embrace the dramatically different culture of this new world order that is emerging into eternity.

Generosity versus greed

Do you like the fact that the first place Jesus went (in John's gospel) was to a party? I like that about Jesus. He goes to the marriage feast and they ran out of wine. If it was me, I would have said, 'All right, who's the bonehead party planner that didn't know how many people were coming? Don't ask me to help him. He'll do it again! I've got to teach this guy a lesson!' Jesus actually did thirty-five hundred plus six-ounce glasses of wine. Do you call that generous? Did you ever look at your career and your chequebook and note that new created order is about generosity, about blessing other people? I've a friend who is a Type A guy who has a Midas touch. Everything he does in the business world turns to tons of money. He said to me, 'Joe, do you know why I'm so passionate about doing my work?' I said, 'No, tell me.' He said, 'To support my habit.' And I said, 'Should we close the door now and you can confess? What's your habit?' He said, 'My habit is giving as much money as I can to advancing the cause of Jesus Christ.' That's an NCPer who knows that investing in eternity is the best investment anybody could ever make.

We can go through the Gospels; hear Christ roll out the dramatically different realities of the new creation and embrace them and live a dramatically different life till everybody who is watching says, 'Why do you do this?' 'Because I'm an NCPer.' And when they ask, 'What does that mean?' you can sit them down and tell them about the wonderful story of the emergent Jesus against the old fallen, damned order of this world and what a privilege it is to be in him, to be a part of it.

It was the passion of the early church that they lived with the confidence that some day the new created order would become fully and finally, totally, a reality. They lived with their eyes fixed on the new day, the new heavens and the new earth. Have your eyes been so taken with the lure of this fallen place? Are you so earthbound that you have forgotten to live, to hope, for that day? If you are in him, if you know where you are, then you know who you are and it has all kinds of significant ramifications for your life.

I've a friend in the States who's a great preacher. His name is Tony Evans. I was sitting there one time being fed by Tony and he made this comment that I will never forget. He said, 'Every one of us ought to be sneak previews of the really big show to come.' That's it in a nutshell. As NCPers we live to be sneak previews of the really big show to come and when you do that, then that is the glory of the gospel through you.

Simply Jesus

Introduction

I want to thank you very much – you have been a delight to teach the word of God to. I've sensed that you have brought open hearts, that you haven't been sitting there thinking, 'I dare you to tell me something I don't know about the Bible.' I've sensed there's been a lot of new covenant sparks flying all week in your hearts and that you'll take that home with you.

Where are we?

I was pastoring in a little town in the USA and my daughter Olivia was about seven at the time. She came to me one day and she said 'Daddy, are we famous?' I said, 'No, Libby, we've not famous.' She paused for a minute and looked at me and said back, 'We would be if more people knew about us!'

Poor Libby, only seven and already struggling with this thing of who recognises us, who affirms us, where do we stand in life and where are we on the social ladder. This thing that we struggle with, probably every single day of our lives, that somehow our world ought to be all about us. Our world doesn't help us with this, does it? When you go into any bookstore and look at the best-seller shelves, inevitably there are books about how to look out for number one, how to put yourself at the top of the pile, how to get ahead in this life even if you have to climb over somebody else. And it doesn't escape the church.

I find it remarkable how often I hear people wandering out of a service saying to somebody, 'I didn't get anything at all out of the message.' I wonder if it ever crossed your fallen little heart that the message was not for you! 'I don't like the music. I'm not singing.' Did it ever cross your you-know-what heart that maybe somebody else has that worship language? We call ourselves followers of Christ; why are we so bound with this horrible disease that life has to be all about us? I want to say this as gently as I can. If life is always all about you, some day you're going to be bored to death. Nobody is special enough to enthral themselves with themselves for the rest of their lives. You're just not that special.

I'm 61 and I'm already getting tired of me. I'm getting tired of those insecurities that have dogged me my whole life, that I try to climb on top of, the insecurities that haunt my spirit almost every single day. I'm tired of those failures that I think I've got on top of and then there they are again, nipping at my soul. I get tired of that, tired of feeling uncomfortable in some situations that I ought to know how to deal with; tired of walking by groups of people who are discussing spiritual things after my message and they're saying, 'Wasn't Dominic Smart great this morning?' I feel tired of the way I feel when those things happen. I'm tired of the awkward way I feel every once in a long while when somebody praises me; I'm tired of not knowing what to do with that. But I'm here to tell you another thing. After all of these years, I still have not grown tired of Jesus. I find him today more compelling, more awesome, more adventuresome, more wonderful, more followable, more sometimes wonderfully troubling, more surprising than I have ever found him in my life. I find that I never get tired of Jesus. And I've also discovered that if life is all about me, it can't be about him. And if it's going to be all about him then it can be nothing of me; I've discovered you can't have it both ways. And if I have to make a choice, I'll choose a life that's all about Jesus. I find such satisfaction in that.

I think that's what Paul must have had in mind when he wrote our text this evening, Philippians chapter 3. Let's see if we can exorcise this nagging demon of our hearts so that we can turn our hearts wonderfully, fully, to Jesus. In Philippians chapter 3:1, Paul writes: 'Finally, my brethren'. I get a real kick out of that, it's so like a preacher, isn't it? 'And now for my last point' – and he's only halfway through his sermon! But actually it's not a time reference. He's saying, 'Finally, my brethren, rejoice in the Lord!' I used to think that was 'Be happy in Jesus all the time!' I'd walk around with a twenty-four-hour smile on my face. Do people like that bother you? People like that bother me. I want to throw the Bible at them and say 'Jesus wept – what do you think about that?'

Thankfully, that's not what this text means. It's not 'Be happy in Jesus all the time.' What it means is 'Stop rejoicing in yourself and start rejoicing in the Lord.' It's going to become very clear in the context that that's where Paul's going with this. If you want to boast, boast in him. Isn't that what Jeremiah chapter 9 says? You know 'Let not the mighty man boast of his might, let not a rich man boast of his riches', but if you want to brag about something, brag on this – that you know God and you are seeking to know him more. That's where Paul's going with this.

Now why would Paul say this to the church at Philippi? It says 'to write the same things again is no trouble for me, and it is a safeguard for you.' Paul can often get a little edgy in his writings and he says 'Beware of the dogs, beware of the evil workers, beware of the false circumcision.' He's talking about a certain group within the New Testament church called the Judaisers. They were Jewish people who had come to know the Lord but forgot to read the book of Hebrews, where we read that Jesus completed all of the Levitical laws. They said in order to be a really class A Christian, you had to keep all the Levitical order; you had to do all the feasts and sacrifices and circumcision. They elevated themselves to be the class A citizens of Christianity and looked down on those who were so pagan that they didn't conform to the Levitical code. Which takes my mind back to what we said earlier: the better you become, the worse you may be. If you really are into the rules game, and you keep all the rules, your

Christianity can easily become all about you. See how subtle this is? 'Look what a good Christian I am.' That's what was going on here. Whereas, in Galatians, Paul goes after their theology, in Philippians he goes after their attitude, because they're walking around saying, 'We are the good Christians in the group.' He goes after those who are boasting in themselves.

In verse 3 he says, 'For we are the true circumcision who worship in the Spirit of God.' Here's the clue: 'we ... who ... glory in Christ Jesus and put no confidence in the flesh, although I myself might have confidence even in the flesh. If anyone else has a mind to put confidence in the flesh, I far more'. Then he brings his credentials. Now quite frankly being in the UK or the USA in 2005 these credentials don't sound all that impressive. But if you were Jewish, back in Paul's day, these are unrivalled credentials. He's saying 'If anybody has the right to boast, it's me.' Look at what he says: he was 'circumcised the eighth day'. That was exactly what the law required, not one day earlier, not one day later. He's saying 'from the very beginning, I was conformed to the law. I am of the nation of Israel, I am of the tribe of Benjamin.' That was the elite tribe, that was the aristocracy. 'I am a Hebrew of the Hebrews. As to the Law, a Pharisee ...' Nobody knew the law better, nobody practised the law better, than the Pharisees. And 'as to zeal, a persecutor of the church; as to righteousness which is in the Law' think about being able to say that 'found blameless ...'

What are our credentials?

I wonder what your credentials are? What is that about you that you feel good about, that you would like to have everybody notice? What's your list of credentials that tempts you to boast in yourself? What have you done with those? A few of you are saying, 'I don't have any credentials and I don't like people who do.' So that's your credential thing; we've all got them. Why it is you feel so put off when people don't affirm and recognise you? Why do you feel absolutely terrific when people notice that stuff about you? What have you done with that? My prayer is that the Spirit will take us around the corner, that the Spirit of God took the apostle Paul around, and that we would walk here with him. He said, 'Whatever things were gain to me, those things I have counted as loss for the sake of Christ. More than that, I count all things to be loss in view of the surpassing value of knowing Christ Jesus my Lord.'

This is an important moment. Stack up whatever those things are in your life and put Jesus there and do a values question. What is of greater value to you? Paul says, 'Jesus is of surpassing value. When I look at Jesus, I count the best things in my life to be like dung.' That is what the text says. Can you think of anything more worthless? But compared to Christ, the greatest things in his life were like that. Have you got there yet? Can you come with Paul? Can the Spirit of God convict you?

Gaining Christ

'I count all things but rubbish in order that I may gain Christ.' Just a little theological backdrop here: there's a theology to gaining Christ. How do you gain Christ? How did you get Christ? One day you knocked at heaven's door, Peter answered and you handed him the list of all the great things that you are. And Peter goes, 'Hey Lord, come here! You are not going to believe who we've got at the gate!' The Lord reads it: 'We need people like you! We've been longing for somebody like you! Come on in!' Is that how it happened? Absolutely not.

I'll tell you how it happened. You came to those bloodstained old rugged timbers and you're carrying all your trophies and do you know what you had to do with all that was gained to you? You had to put them down. Did you have to take them off? Did you have to leave them in a stack here? Did you have to stand, looking at the cross, naked before God, in your sinful fallen offensive self and plead, plead mercy at those bloodstained timbers? 'Lord, Lord, I'm so unworthy, I am such a sinner.' As he always does, thank God, he reached down on that day, do you remember it? He touched you with his mercy. He brought you to himself and forgave you and made you his own. And you moved to this side of the cross because of Jesus.

But our problem is that once we get here, we look back at that pile of trophies, don't we? When nobody's looking, we start picking them up again and start wearing them as though they were more important than Jesus. Why? How can we do that to the mercy and grace of God? We had to come with nothing, we had to count all this lost, in order to gain Christ, 'for by grace ye are saved, through faith and it is not of yourself; it is a gift of God'. You brought no merit at all. Why do we walk around the kingdom as though our merit means so much to us, when the kingdom is about the King, Jesus Christ? That's what Paul brings to us. That's the point of conviction, the point of repentance, to go back again to the cross and put that stuff back on the other side of the cross. Turn your eyes and make it all about him, the one of this surpassing value.

'So that I may gain Christ, and may be found in Him, not having a righteousness of my own derived from the Law, but that which is through faith in Christ, the righteousness which comes from God on the basis of faith' and you have to go to verse 11 here, I think that verse 10 is parenthetical, 'in order that I may attain to the resurrection of the dead.' Do you realise that not one of your credentials will get you home to heaven? It is only Jesus that takes you all the way home. Like we said the other night, if he's on your passport there's no hassle at the border. Nothing that you carry makes any difference there.

He says, 'In order that I may attain to the resurrection of the dead, that I may know him.' Verse 10 intrigues me. He says, 'that I may know him'. We've a switch in the Greek words here. We move to the Greek word that means to know by experience 'that I might have intimacy with Christ'. Paul knew what we must know, that coming to Jesus Christ is not about some gift of eternal life. Christ intended it to be deeper than that. It is about a relationship with Jesus Christ. Is there anybody here that longs for deeper, richer intimacy with Jesus Christ? That's a signal of your redemption, he planted that longing in your heart. Paul says, 'that I might know him.' He's saying, 'I'm not satisfied with cognitive knowledge of Christ.' Could that be our problem? If you've grown up in the church world, you probably know a lot about Christology and a lot about Jesus Christ. It's all head knowledge. We know about his divinity, we know about his atonement, we know everything about Jesus. Can I welcome you to a relationship with Jesus? To something down, deep inside, that satisfies the longings of your heart? That's what Paul does; he says, 'I've put everything away, that I might not only gain him but might experience him in my life.' He knew you couldn't have it both ways.

How do you experience Christ?

He unlocks this for us. He says, 'There are three places that you meet Christ, where intimacy is cultivated and enjoyed.' Three places where we 'may know him and the power of his resurrection' (verse 10). The power of God's resurrection is a phenomenal thing. Think about dying and your molecules turning to dust and then God reassembling that in a re-engineered body for eternity. Isn't that miraculous? Are you getting the point that the resurrection is a powerful thing? But this text isn't talking about the resurrection day, because it's in the present tense. It's talking about resurrection power right now. We experience in Christ in his resurrection power in our lives: what on earth does that mean? What was the resurrection? The resurrection was God's final blow against sin and Satan and death and hell. Death was done, sin was done and life was possible in Jesus Christ.

Seduction

Where do you meet his resurrection power, if resurrection power is about putting a nail in sin and Satan and death and hell? It's in those seasons of seduction, those times of temptation, where you are beckoned by sin and Satan and hell and death. It is there that Jesus meets you. It is there that he reaches down his hand, as you lift your heart and say, 'God help me, help me!' He lifts his hand and as you reach yours up, he rescues you from that time of seduction, from that moment of temptation and lets you walk in the power of life, not in the dredges of death and sin. Is that a surprise to you, that you experience Jesus in temptation? He's right here with all of his resurrection power in his hand, reaching out to meet you, to draw you out to victory. Isn't that why we pray in the Lord's Prayer, 'and lead us not into temptation, but deliver us from evil, for thine is the kingdom and the power and the glory'? It's in times of seduction that you meet Jesus Christ and experience his power, as you yield to him and permit him to rescue you.

Suffering

I find it interesting that Paul says, 'I've learned to experience Jesus in the midst of suffering.' There are only three types of people. Those who *have* experienced suffering, those of you who *are* experiencing it, and those of you who *will*. I guess we all are aware of the fact that we have a problem because our first tendency in midst of suffering is to say, 'Get me out of here. God, I hate this. Why are you doing this to me?' Some of us even harden our hearts and turn our fists into his face. Paul says, 'No. For if God brings suffering to you, you meet Jesus there. There is a fellowship to your sufferings.' Is there anybody here who has been lonely? Is there anybody here who has suffered great physical pain? Anybody here who has ever been misunderstood? Anybody here whose been unfairly criticised? Anybody here who has been betrayed by a close friend in whom you have poured your life?

When that loneliness engulfs your soul, it is an important moment for you to have a shared experience with Jesus Christ. Of course you want it to leave. I hope it does leave, but until it does, could you say to Jesus 'Lord, I never ever knew before what it meant for you to love me because now I feel the loneliness you must have felt on that cross for me. I want to meet you here, I want to share in your experience. I love you. You volunteered loneliness for me. Lord, I hate being betrayed by my friend. But, Lord, how you must have felt in that garden, when you started toward the cross for me.' Paul says, 'When suffering comes my way, I meet Jesus there and I share in the fellowship. I experience Jesus in a way I've never experienced him before.'

Surrender

The third place that intimacy with Jesus deepens and grows is at the end of verse 10, 'being conformed to his death'. You say, 'I'll never be crucified.' It's bigger than that. The pattern of his death began in eternity past, with the eternal decree where the Son was assigned to go to the cross and all of that surrender, through all of time, comes to fullness in the Garden of Gethsemane. You've got to see Jesus' human side here. He knows what's coming, and he pleads with the Father, 'God, this is too hard for me.' He is in such anxiety that the little corpuscles that surround the sweat glands are bursting. As he knelt at that rock, he's saying, 'God, you're creative, you're the great Creator, you could get a different plan. Can we please have a different plan?' In that moment, in that garden, at that rock, your friend and brother, Jesus, in that agony, finally through these parched lips we hear these words fall; 'But God, not my will but thine be done.' Surrender. Surrender.

If you wonder why Jesus seems so far away, maybe it's because you've run from the hard stuff he has called you to do. Did you refuse to forgive that person? I know that sometimes God's perfect will is hard. We live in a fallen place among a fallen race. It's not going to be easy. This thing is not a cake walk. It's going to be hard, a lot of times, to do what God wants you to do. And it's in those sweet moments of surrender that he meets you, when you kneel with him at the rock in Gethsemane.

Paul says, 'It is the passion of my life to experience Christ, to have intimacy with Christ.' I'm going, 'Me too, how do I do that?' He says, 'I'll tell you. You meet him in seduction, and you experience him there; you meet him in suffering and you fellowship with the pain he bore for you; and you meet him in surrender. And the more you meet him in those three places, the deeper and richer Jesus will be to you.' But if life is all about you, you'll want to fail in the seduction, won't you? You'll want to fall to temptation. Temptation is very attractive and if life is all about you and making you happy, then you don't want to meet Jesus there. If life is all about you, suffering will be bad, and you'll say, 'I don't deserve this. I'm a better person than this. I know a lot of bad people who ought to have this. How come I've got this suffering?' If life's all about you, that's how you'll feel. And if life is all about you, you'll never kneel in those hard times at that rock with Jesus in Gethsemane. Look what you've missed; the surpassing value of not just having Jesus but experiencing him: intimacy with the friend of your soul. Look at what you've missed, the joy of life with Jesus.

I was having dinner couple of years ago and happened to be seated right next to Billy Graham. I have to tell you the name so you can catch the weight of this. What do you do when you're sitting next to Billy Graham? I said, 'Billy, in all of your ministry, what has brought you the greatest joy? What have you loved the most about your life?' Then, as though he wouldn't be able to think of anything, I started supplying answers for him. I said, 'Maybe it's hanging out with kings and powerful people, being a friend to every president and praying with them.' I was going to get a little more spiritual and say, 'Or is it preaching the gospel to literally millions of people all over the world?' I didn't get that far because he took his hand across the linen table-cloth as though to wipe all of my lame suggestions on the floor. He said, 'Joe, it's none of that.' And without rehearsal, spontaneously, he said, 'Joe, by far and away, the highest joy of my life has been my fel-lowship with Jesus.' Then, just in case I missed it, he said, 'I just have to tell you, there is nothing else; the highest joy of my life has been my fellowship with Jesus.' Then he filled in the blanks: 'To know that he was there with me, to have him speak to me, to have him minister to me, to have him be the guide of my life ...' He just went on and on and I felt convicted and challenged all at the same time.

I felt convicted because I wasn't sure I could say that. I felt chal-lenged that when I'm eighty, I want to say that. Some of you are say-ing, 'Yeah but that's Billy Graham, God's anointed one ... I'm nobody.' All right. Let me tell you about my grandmother. My grand-mother was a farmer's wife in southern Michigan. Her whole life was spent keeping the house and cooking meals for the farmhands. Nobody outside of this little, small group of friends ever knew her name, she was never in the limelight and she gave birth to two chil-dren in a clapboard home. My dad was born in the upstairs bedroom in January and they had to fill rags into the cracks between the win-dows to keep the cold air from coming into that little baby's new bedroom. She was nobody. I can still remember her saying to me, 'Little Joe, do you know what my favourite hymn is?' I can still remember hearing her sing this around the house. And I'd say, 'No, Grandma, what's your favourite hymn?' She'd start singing it. The words go like this. 'I come to the garden alone, while the dew is still on the roses, and the voice I hear falling on my ear, the Son of God, the Son of God this close is. And he walks with me and he talks with me and he tells me I'm his own and the joy we share as we tarry there none other has ever known.'

If it's good enough for Billy Graham, if it's that wonderful for my grandmother, then it's for me and it's for you. When you seek Jesus by giving all of yourself away, and making him the passionate pursuit, meeting him in seduction, and in suffering and in surrender, you too will know the joy of Jesus and that's part of the glory of the gospel.

Preaching the word

by Peter Maiden

PETER MAIDEN

Keswick's current Chairman and the International Director of Operation Mobilisation, Peter is a very busy man! He travels extensively to fulfil his commitments with OM, overseeing the day to day co-ordination of its ministry in 82 countries worldwide. Peter is also an elder at Hebron Evangelical church in Carlisle, where he lives, and manages to include itinerant Bible teaching in the UK and overseas into his schedule.

Peter enjoys family life with his wife Win and their three children and four grandchildren. As well as endurance sports, in particular he loves long distance running, fell walking and long distance cycling.

Preaching the word

Acts 2

Introduction

I have been reading, over the past few months, a book which has disturbed me very greatly. It's a book authored by Ron Sider and it's called *The Scandal of the Evangelical Conscience*.[2] And Sider shows, using polling work from such people as Gallup and Barna, that there is very little difference between the number of evangelical Christian married couples who divorce their spouses and those completely outside of the church. He reports that, according to the polls, the most likely group in American society to complain about having neighbours from another ethnic group are white evangelicals. Those are two statements from this deeply disturbing book. It is true that towards the end of the book, Sider shows that when it comes to what he describes as totally committed believers, the picture is slightly better; but only slightly.

Now a number of things can be said about this. Firstly, recent experiences in the political field show that we shouldn't totally trust these polls and, of course, this is commenting on the scene in North America and not Europe. But having recognised all of that, if these

[2] Ronald Sider, *The scandal of the evangelical conscience* (Baker Books, 2005)

polls are even half accurate, what we have here is a frightening and a truly disturbing situation. Another book tells us that 20 per cent of Christians in America believe in reincarnation and 26 per cent believe in astrology. I must say that I came away from reading those books thinking: 'To what degree have these people who consider themselves to be evangelicals really understood the gospel?' It reminds me of the title of a book that was popular a few years ago: *Are evangelicals born again?*[3] This of course leads to a second question: 'Is the gospel being proclaimed in our churches a biblical gospel?' Is it a glorious gospel or are we in danger of offering just another self-help programme or self-improvement technique?

The Acts of the Apostles

In these evening meetings we're going to look into the Acts of the Apostles, at selected passages which will show the growth of the gospel in the church's earliest days. And the Acts of the Apostles is a truly fascinating book.

There is, of course, a great debate about what the title of the book should really be. Is it really the Acts of the Apostles? Apart from Paul, only three apostles are actually mentioned in the book. Is this not more the Acts of the Holy Spirit? Certainly in this book the mighty power of the Spirit is clearly seen but the human instruments, the apostles, are also a vital part of this story. That's I think where we must begin.

We see in these early chapters the church, ordinary men and women, transformed by the power of the Spirit. They were a bunch paralysed by fear but as Luke explains in chapter 1:3, Jesus, after his suffering, showed himself to them and he gave them convincing proofs that he was alive. They saw the risen Christ. Then they heard his message and it was this: 'Do not leave Jerusalem,' (Acts 1:4) 'wait for the gift my Father promised ... in a few days' (verse 5) 'you will be baptised with the Holy Spirit.' And when that takes place (verse 8)

---

[3] R Kent Hughes, *Are evangelicals born again – the character traits of true faith* (Crossway Books, 1995)

'you will be my witnesses' ... 'Start in Jerusalem, move to Judea, then Samaria and to the ends of the earth.'

Here in chapter 2, our passage for this evening, that promise is fulfilled. The Lord Jesus, now exalted to his Father's right hand, performs the last work of his saving career, at least until his coming again; and that last work is to pour out the Holy Spirit on his waiting followers and a new day begins. God's kingdom is inaugurated.

Equipped for ministry

As John Stott points out in his commentary on Acts,

> Just as Luke records in chapter 3 of his gospel the Spirit coming on Jesus, equipping him for public ministry, now here in Acts he records the fact of the Spirit coming on his people to equip them and to equip us for ministry. What is that ministry? It is to proclaim throughout the world the great news of the gospel.[4]

I want you first of all to note this simple point: the church, transformed by the Spirit, is immediately thrust out in witness. The disciples can no longer spend their time looking intently into the sky, as they did in chapter 1:10, looking for a glimpse of their now ascended Lord. No. There's work to be done. It is a work of the Holy Spirit but it's a work in which the Holy Spirit will involve the church and his intention is to involve every church member, every believer. It's the work of taking this glorious gospel to the peoples of the world.

That's actually what we have in this book of Acts. One commentator has suggested that an appropriate title for the book would be *How the gospel was brought from Jerusalem to Rome*, and it is a remarkable story. A religion – if you'll allow me to call Christianity that – begins in a little corner of Palestine and within thirty years it reaches Rome, the capital of the world; from the capital of the Jews to the capital of the world in record-breaking time. This is the power of the gospel; this

---

4 John Stott, *The message of Acts, The Bible speaks today series* (Leicester: IVP, 1994)

is the power of the Spirit. Paul's words in Romans 1:16 are a sort of commentary on this. You recall he writes 'I'm not ashamed of the gospel, because it's the power of God for the salvation of everyone who believes; first for the Jew and then for the Gentile.' As he writes in the previous verse, he's so convinced of the gospel's power that he's eager to get to Rome. 'I must preach the gospel in Rome, the centre of power, that's where I want to be, and that's where I want to take this glorious gospel.'

A missionary church

I don't want to move on from this point until we clearly have it in our minds, until we have faced its challenge both for ourselves and for our churches. The church transformed by the Spirit is immediately thrust out into witness. And they are not to rest until their witness is known throughout the world. Stott quotes Henry Boer in his book *Pentecost and Missions*.[5] 'The Acts,' writes Boer,

> is governed by one dominant, overriding, all-controlling motif. This motif is the expansion of the faith through missionary witness in the power of the Spirit. Restlessly the Spirit drives the church to witness and continually churches rise out of the witness. The church is a missionary church. Is yours? Is mine? Are you and I mission-minded individuals? Because the Holy Spirit who indwells us is a missionary Spirit.' Are we quenching him? Are we gazing into the heavens when there's work to be done?

May I just emphasise this point once more and then I will move on. At the end of the chapter we have this wonderful picture of the church (verse 42). 'They devoted themselves to the apostles' teaching and the fellowship, to the breaking of bread and to prayer.' I'm sure you must have heard at least one sermon on that verse, telling you that that verse contains the elements of healthy church life but if you're ever going to preach such a sermon from that verse, will you please

---

[5] Henry Boer, *Pentecost and Missions* (Eerdmans, 1964)

add on the end of verse 47: 'The Lord added to their number daily those who were being saved.' Yes, these early Christians certainly devoted themselves to learning and sharing and worshipping but not to the degree that they forgot about witnessing. Clearly they were a witnessing community and God was blessing their witness. Maybe it's time for a review. How many of the activities of your church involve Christians actually witnessing to those who are not yet Christians? Maybe it's a cause for a life review. How many of the things that I do, in the goodness of God, may lead to opportunities to witness to those who are not yet Christians?

A number of years ago we engaged in an exercise in Operation Mobilisation. We asked ourselves this question: 'What is the critical event in our ministry?' And we concluded that that critical event was reached when one of us – any one of us – was standing with a person who is not yet a Christian and was sharing the love of Christ with that person. Then we looked at every aspect of our work and we asked this: how can we increase the number of those critical events taking place? We can do many good things in our lives, many great things in our churches but I say, maybe for the last time this evening, the church transformed by the Spirit was thrust out immediately in witness.

The day of Pentecost

Now let's get back to Acts 2. It is an amazing scene. A noise, probably something like a tornado, rushes through the room where the disciples are waiting. Eugene Peterson in *The Message* describes it like this: 'Without warning there was a sound like a strong wind, gale force – no one could tell where it came from. It filled the whole building. Then, like a wildfire, the Holy Spirit spread through their ranks, and they started speaking in a number of different languages as the Spirit prompted them.'

The gift of languages was especially significant at this time. It was Pentecost, the celebration of the grain harvest and Jerusalem was thronged with Jews. According to verse 5, they came 'from every nation under heaven'.

We don't know exactly what happened next. Did these Jews hear the commotion going on inside the room? Or did the disciples, in their excitement, burst out of the room? Whichever way it was, it seems a street meeting began. This was a street meeting with a difference. The hearers were clearly from many different language groups yet each one heard these apostles speaking in their own language. Surely this is an underlining of what we've already seen. 'This message is to go to all peoples, yes, starting here in Jerusalem but don't stop here, the ends of the earth are your destination; my kingdom is to be a multi-racial kingdom, it's to be a multi-lingual kingdom.'

There's a little glimpse here of what John saw in a vision, people from every tribe and every tongue and every nation worshipping the Lamb, eternally. There's a very important progression here. The transformed church is thrust out in witness, but what is that witness? They are to bring the word of God to the people, verse 11, 'they declared the wonders of God'. That's our task: to declare the truth about God and to do it in the language of the people.

A few months ago I was in Thailand at the triannual meetings of Wycliffe SIL and I was hearing of their vision, along with other Bible translation groups, to have the Scriptures in every necessary language by the year 2025. It's a fabulous vision; there's something special about hearing the gospel in your native tongue. And I don't think it's stretching this incident too far to take from it not just the challenge to proclaim the gospel, to preach the word of God, but the challenge to do it in a way that people can truly understand. We have this constant challenge as Christian communicators and it's a double-header; we are to be faithful to the truth but we are to be constantly considering ways to apply that truth which are relevant and meaningful to our hearers. It is a glorious gospel; and one reason it's so glorious is that it meets the deepest needs of human beings. We must be praying constantly for the skill to apply the medicine of the gospel effectively.

Proclaiming the word of God

Some were apparently not impressed by this witness (verse 13). 'Some however made fun of them and said, "They have had too much wine."' But Peter will not be put off by this cynicism. He sees it as an opportunity, he raises his voice and he says (verse 16). 'This is that' –

that's how the AV translates it – 'which was spoken by the prophet Joel.'

So my second very simple point is that the church, transformed by the Spirit, proclaimed the word of God in her witness. The sermon which Peter now preaches from verse 14 down to verse 39 is packed full with Scripture. Peter is expounding Old Testament Scripture as the basis of his witness. He's explaining what is happening – by relating the events to Scripture. He's telling them what they must do – by referring them to Scripture. Here in Acts 2 we have a demonstration of the power of the Holy Spirit using God's Word through a human instrument. I believe in a holistic approach to mission. I believe God is interested, he's concerned for people as a whole: body, mind and spirit. I believe he's concerned to see communities in which people are living transformed lives but I believe that we, as the people of God, have a particular responsibility to convey the word of God to the people and if we don't do that, who will?

A second evaluation question we might ask ourselves and we might ask in our churches is this: to what degree is 'This is that' the theme of our witness? To what extent is our witness based around bringing people back to the word; explaining life from God's word, pointing out actions required of people from God's word? When the work of the Holy Spirit is quite rightly being given a huge emphasis in the church, if in such a day we see a neglect of the word of God, we've lost the plot. We're actually deceiving ourselves. And here's a marvellous example. When the Holy Spirit is truly at work, he will use ordinary men and women to proclaim his word. And I would go so far as to say that a clear sign of a true work of the Spirit is where Christ is exalted, through the Holy Spirit, by using men and women who proclaim his word.

What did the apostles teach?

Let's look briefly at this sermon Peter preached, because it's a wonderful proclamation of the glory of God. As we do that we need to recognise that the book of Acts is full of sermons. John Stott discovered no less than nineteen significant speeches in this book, stating that the title of the book might just as well have been *The Addresses of the Apostles* as *The Acts of the Apostles*. These apostles certainly were preachers of the Word. So what did they preach? Look at the sermon with me and notice some crucial themes.

History has meaning

First of all, they taught there is a sense to history. Peter very strongly presents Jesus and all that happened to Jesus as the fulfilment of Old Testament prophecy. In doing that he's saying to his hearers that history is not haphazard. God is at work in his world. The Sovereign of the universe is in control and he is working out his purpose as year succeeds to year. In a day of increasing pessimism about life and an increasing hopelessness about the future, this is a crucial element of our gospel, a crucial element of our good news. In verses 22 and 23, Peter declares that the cross – which might have been seen as the great moment of failure, a particular moment of chaos – was right in line with the great purpose of God. Verse 23: 'This man was handed over to you by God's set purpose and foreknowledge.' In emphasising this, Peter is also saying God is faithful. God keeps his promises. For four hundred years, people had been waiting for the fulfilment of Joel's prophecy and God has kept his word; the Holy Spirit has been released exactly as Joel predicted. This is good news; the faithful God is at the heart of his world and he is working out his holy and good purposes.

The Messiah has come

Secondly, they taught that in Jesus the Messiah has come; the new age has dawned. God sent Jesus, he was crucified by wicked men, yes, but as part of God's set purpose. God raised Jesus from the dead; God has exalted Jesus, God has made him Lord and Christ. In other words, Peter is saying that God has entered the human arena, eternity has invaded time. The world can never be the same again.

If God is in control of history, then Jesus is the hinge of history. This new age is a wonderful age, as you can see from Joel's prophecy. Twice the promise, 'I will pour out my Spirit' is made. Are you expecting showers of blessing? I think the statement here suggests much more than that. His Spirit, says Peter, will be poured out in these days. It's a statement of abundance, it's a statement of generosity; and as we see the amazing turning to Christ around the world, you see this prophecy being fulfilled before our eyes.

It'll also be an age of upheavals, says Peter, verse 20: 'The sun will be turned to darkness, the moon to blood.' This could be literal; such things had only recently been witnessed on Good Friday, but this would also have been a normal way in that day of describing times of political and social upheaval. Right now in India we're in the middle of a huge social upheaval, as the Dalits, the Untouchables, that's the name they give themselves, the lowest of the low in India, are leaving Hinduism by the million. Many of them are entering Buddhism but about a million have entered the Christian church in India, just in the last two years. And God is pouring out his Spirit in this time of social upheaval. In our own organisation, Operation Mobilisation, we've seen fifteen hundred churches established amongst the Dalits in the last two years.

Note again that in this age there'll be an emphasis on prophecy, proclamation: there'll be visions, there'll be dreams, there'll be prophecy. Why? All with the purpose of making known the glory of God. It will be an age of wonderful opportunity because (verse 21) 'Everyone who calls on the name of the Lord will be saved.' It will be an age which moves constantly forwards towards a climax (verse 20), 'the coming of the great and glorious day of the Lord'. The Lord who is in control of history has placed a fixed time for this age with a glorious climax.

There is much talked today, as we know, about the new age movement but the reality is that Christ inaugurated the new age more than two thousand years ago. This is a crucial element of our gospel; to proclaim that the God who is in control of history has entered the human arena in Christ and today is a day of mercy, generosity and opportunity because it's the age of the Spirit, when everyone who calls on the name of the Lord will be saved. Their message was there's a meaning to history and in Jesus the Messiah has come; the new age has dawned.

They preached Christ

As Peter begins to explain Joel's prophecy in verse 22, his first word is 'Jesus'… 'Men of Israel, hear these words: Jesus of Nazareth' … As he brings his sermon to a climax, his challenge in verse 38 is this: 'Repent and be baptised every one of you in the name of Jesus Christ.' If Jesus is the hinge of history, the inaugurator of this new age, then Jesus will be the theme of their preaching. Yes, they preach the word but they actually preach Christ through the word. Peter speaks of his life, he speaks of his work, he speaks of his death and the whole sermon is really about his resurrection. He speaks of an eternal Lord who rules over heaven and earth.

One further evaluation question. Are we preaching Christ? Is there enough preaching today from the Gospels? Are we telling the gospel story over and over again, are we exalting Christ, his person, his work, his resurrection, his ascended glory? Verse 36, 'Let all the house of Israel be assured of this: God has made this Jesus, whom you crucified, both Lord and Christ.'

Repentance

They preached, fourthly, repentance and the gift of the Spirit. Such preaching got a response. Verse 37, 'When they heard this, they were cut to the heart and they said to Peter and the other apostles, "Brothers, what shall we do?"' And the answer is clear: 'Repent and be baptised.' Repent: a complete change of thinking, a complete change of direction. That takes me back to where I began, to this book by Ron Sider. When people who claim to be evangelical in their thinking and action are so similar to society around them, you have to ask whether repentance is being preached and, if it is, whether it's being understood.

If we're going to be faithful to God and to his Word and truly faithful to our listeners, we must preach the necessity of repentance. Peter is very clear about the death of Christ (verse 23), 'Christ was handed over to you by God's set purpose and foreknowledge, but you – you – with the help of wicked men, you put him to death, you nailed him to the cross.'

Peter wants these people to face up to their sin. He wants to show them how they used to think about Christ and the need to think about him and act towards him in an entirely different way. In other words, he wants them to repent. Baptism will be a clear public statement of their repentance, because they'll be baptised into the name of the Father, the Son and the Holy Spirit. The one they have previously rejected so violently: they'll now be publicly baptised into his name. And what a promise for those who repent – forgiveness and power; the power of the Holy Spirit. What a hopeless call the call to repentance would be without this twofold promise of forgiveness and the gift of the Spirit. How well I know, and I'm sure you know, our utter inability to change our thinking and our actions but the promise of power is ours: forgiveness for the past, and the power of the Spirit for the present and for the future. How vital that we proclaim, as the response to this glorious gospel, the necessity of repentance, the reality of forgiveness and the promise of power.

I'm not at all surprised that Luke follows his report of Peter's sermon and the response of the people with this beautiful picture of the church (verses 42-47). For this is essential to our gospel. We're not converted to live isolated lives. We're converted to be part of this new community growing together, learning together. A statement from Lesslie Newbigin has impacted me greatly in recent years. He wrote this:

> The deepest root of the contemporary malaise of Western culture is an individualism which denies the fundamental reality of our human nature as given by God – namely that we grow into true humanity only in relationships of faithfulness and responsibility toward one another. The local congregation is called to be and by the grace of God often is, such a community. When it is, it stands in the wider community of the neighbourhood and nation not primarily as the promoter of programmes for social change (although it will be that) but primarily the church stands, as itself, the foretaste of a different social order.

The glory of gospel

We must appreciate that, today, people are coming to our churches looking for that; they're coming looking for community. I didn't say committees; they're coming looking for community. What a subject we've got before us – the glory of the gospel. The church transformed by the Spirit, proclaims this gospel uncompromisingly; persecution will not silence her, cynicism will not lead to any diluting of the truth. I trust we'll be blessed again as we see the true glory of this gospel, the wonder of our salvation, but I also trust we'll remember that we are blessed to be a blessing. So let us commit not just to enjoy this gospel personally and collectively, but to get out there into these communities and live out and proclaim the true glory of this fabulous message and let's not stop until we've reached the ends of the earth.

Dying to live

by Liam Goligher

LIAM GOLIGHER

Liam Goligher has been Senior Pastor of Duke Street Baptist church in Richmond, Surrey, since April 2000. He has also pastored churches in Ireland, Canada and in his native Scotland, where he saw significant church growth as the pastor of Kirkintilloch Baptist church in Glasgow. After studying at the Irish Baptist College, Liam pursued post-graduate work at the University of Waterloo, Canada, and at the Reformed Theological Society, Jackson, Mississippi, where he has recently completed his PhD. His teaching is heard weekly on Premier radio, Sky Digital and Freeview. His Duke Street ministry is available online at <u>www.dukestreetchurch.com</u>.

Liam has contributed to a number of books as well as writing two of his own: *Window on Tomorrow*, which looks at the practical aspects of the Second Coming of Christ, and *The Fellowship of the King,* which looks at the New Testament vision of the new community as an answer to the loneliness and alienation that we see in Western society.

Liam is a Trustee of the Keswick Ministries. He is married to Christine, and they have five children, two grandchildren and a Bedlington terrier!

Dying to live

Acts 7

Introduction

They say that something is only worth living for if it's worth dying for. And when the crunch comes and death stares you in the face, you better be sure that you're living for the right thing. The first Christian martyr, Stephen, teaches us this lesson.

In the seventh chapter we're confronted with something unique in the book of Acts. It's a record of Stephen's speech, an apologia from the end of his trial. The authorities were accusing him of speaking words of blasphemy against Moses and against God (Acts 6:11). Stephen was one of the seven chosen by the apostles (Acts 6:1-7), when they were being distracted from their gospel ministry; full of the Spirit and wisdom. 'Stephen, a man full of God's grace and power, did great wonders and miraculous signs among the people' (Acts 7:8). That description is almost unique in the book of Acts as a description of someone who wasn't one of the apostles. It's there to grab our attention. We are to take this man very seriously.

Where did his troubles all begin? They all began with a theological debate (Acts 6:9). Stephen – his name is a Greek name – was a Hellenistic Jew, that is a Jew from a Greek background, and he went to the Greek-speaking synagogue in Jerusalem. He'd been converted and as he started talking openly about his Christian faith (verse 10), the people who were arguing with him could not stand up against his wisdom or the Spirit by whom he spoke. And they were irritated. If you've ever been in an argument with someone who keeps winning, you can imagine the aggravation that they felt. Every argument they brought up, every Bible reference that they quoted, was countered by this man who had such a grasp of the Bible.

In verse 11, we're told that they were so furious with him, they secretly persuaded some people to act as false witnesses and to say these false words, 'We heard Stephen speak words of blasphemy against Moses and against God. This fellow never stops speaking against the temple and against the law.' That's where it all begins and it goes downhill from there.

We have to take Stephen and his speech seriously for a number of reasons. First of all, if you look at the length of the speech in chapter 7, it's the longest speech recorded in the book of Acts. It's longer than Peter's sermon on the day of Pentecost; longer than any of Paul's defences or sermons. Then if you look at the style of it, it's not a sermon in the normally accepted understanding of a sermon. It doesn't expound any particular Scripture; instead, he gives a summary of the Old Testament, a bird's eye view of the big picture and he explains where that Scripture is heading. And if you look at the outcome of his sermon, it contributes to the impact that is being made on the apostle Paul, Saul, who's standing by as the witnesses throw their stones. It (Chapter 8) leads to a unique and dramatic growth in the life of the church as the church is pushed out beyond the boundaries of Jerusalem into Judea and Samaria, and then Africa is impacted by the overspill.

What is going on here? Stephen is a man on fire and he understands very clearly, as we must, that at this stage in the story of redemption, it is the Christian church and the Christian message that is on trial with him before the highest court in Judaism. Stephen is standing before men and God as a witness.[6] He is a martyr; the Greek

---

[6] In the context of the book he is presented as a witness. In strictly legal terms he is the accused. In the sight of God he is a witness and indirectly witnesses to the illegality of the proceedings.

word *marturio* means a witness, and at this stage it doesn't mean what we mean by the word martyr; at least not yet. It will do by the time Stephen's story is done.

Stephen is on trial for something that he did not do. But in the course of this speech he explains what he really believes, and what he really believes is far more serious. It's like a man who's on trial for burglary and the judge says, 'This is the accusation against you: you are guilty of breaking into 42 Victoria Gardens.' And the man says, 'Your Honour, I'm not guilty of that; I didn't ever break in or steal anything. But I broke into the Bank of England and took away all the gold reserves.' Stephen's saying, 'What you've brought up as a charge is a false charge. Let me tell you what it is I believe and what I've really been teaching.'

Stephen: a witness to Israel

Stephen dies for the difference between Judaism's approach to God and Christianity's. This is a transitional time, in the book of Acts, as Christianity is beginning to find itself in conflict with Judaism, and the real issues are identified. Up until this time, the Christians had been Jewish by background or by conversion. They've observed all the Jewish festivals, they've seen Christianity as the natural fulfilment of Judaism and at this point are still regarded as a sect within Judaism. But it cannot remain like that if this new movement is to fulfil Jesus' commission.

The religious leaders, however, are beginning to get concerned about this. Reports are coming to them that Christianity is raising questions against the temple and the law. That's the charge that's brought against Stephen. Now to understand that, you need to know that in the Old Testament and in Jesus' day, the Jewish people regarded the temple and the law and the land as being of central significance in the purposes of God. The temple was the place where you met with God, the law was that in which God revealed himself and the land was the Promised Land. They were the demarcation boundaries within which God operated. He did not operate outside of them. That's why their charge is so significant. Stephen, they said, is teaching that 'Jesus of Nazareth will destroy this place' – that is the temple – 'and change the customs that Moses handed down to us.' Stephen, in his defence, deals with the issues that they have raised – the temple and the law. We'll see as we go on how relevant these are to us.

The people

Stephen says: 'God has not tied himself to a place, he has tied himself to his people.' He believes in progressive revelation, that God has revealed himself over time incrementally, bit by bit, at different times in different ways, to different people. Stephen wasn't alive to write the epistle to the Hebrews but it echoes so much of what he says in this speech. Hebrews begins like this: 'In times past God spoke to our forefathers through the prophets at various times and in various ways'. Stephen picks up that idea.

Abraham

He begins with Abraham, the father of faith. 'The God of glory,' he says, 'appeared to our father Abraham while he was still in Mesopotamia, before he lived in Haran.' The God of glory, the God who has weight, the God who is splendid in himself, who is the one to be taken seriously in all the universe, the one who reveals himself to his people, the God of glory revealed himself to Abraham. And where did he reveal himself to Abraham? Was it in the Promised Land? Was it in the temple?

No! God revealed himself to Abraham in Haran, which was far away from the Promised Land, years before there ever was a temple. While Abraham was still an unbeliever and a sun-worshipper, a pagan man, God revealed himself to him. While he was in Mesopotamia, while his family still worshipped other gods, while they were far from the Promised Land, God spoke to Abraham and called him to himself.

Joseph

Stephen goes on to tell the story of Joseph and he emphasises the surprising context in which God was with Joseph. It was in Egypt; in fact he mentions the word Egypt six times in seven verses. Egypt was a dirty word to Jews and so Stephen emphasises it over and over again: where was it, he says, that God worked such a miracle of grace? It was in Egypt. It was in Egypt that God secured the prosperity of Joseph. It was in Egypt that God made Joseph a ruler of the people, the saviour of Israel. It was in Egypt that Jacob, his father, eventually died. It was in Egypt that the family of Israel was to expand and grow great and become a nation in itself. It was in Egypt, the very watchword of paganism, that God moved in the life of Joseph.

Moses

What about Moses? Stephen tells them that it was in Egypt that Moses appears as the great leader and deliverer of his people. He's born in Egypt. It was in Egypt that his own people did not recognise him. So he leaves and goes to the desert, verse 30, and God appears to him in the burning bush near Mount Sinai. It was not in the holy land that God said to Moses, 'Take off your shoes, for the ground on which you stand is holy ground.' It wasn't in the temple that God said, 'This is holy ground.' It was in the desert, among a pagan tribe. As John Stott puts it: 'This statement is central to Stephen's thesis. There was holy ground outside of the holy land, for wherever God is, is holy.' In fact, Stephen goes on, 'Where did God hear the oppression of his people? It was while they were still in Egypt.' While they were far from the Promised Land, God heard their cry and it registered with him. In other words, God's mercies, his compassion, love and grace towards his people are not tied either to a temple or to a land. God's presence and God's compassion over-rule it all. Where did God give the law, the word that he gave to Moses, the living words, the oracles of God that he refers to in verses 37 and 38? They were given outside of the Promised Land, as the Israelites were going through the desert.

David and Solomon

Then Stephen goes on a tour of the Old Testament; to the reigns of David and Solomon where the transition takes place from a tabernacle or a tent to the temple – from a mobile home to a fixed sanctuary. At the inauguration of the temple, King Solomon acknowledges that not even the highest heaven could contain God, 'much less this house that my hands have built.' Stephen draws this conclusion: 'The Most High does not live in houses made by men.' Stephen's point is this: God is transcendent. 'What you have done,' he's saying, 'is you have taken God and put him in a box. You have tied him to a place and a land. You don't understand that God, the living God of Israel, is so great and so transcendent he cannot stay within the bounds you have created. His presence cannot be localised; no building can ever contain him; no power of man can ever inhibit him. He is not tied down anywhere except to his people to whom he has made covenant promises.'

The law

Then Stephen talks about the law and he says God has tied himself to his word. He's been accused of disrespecting the law of Moses, but he asks them who it was that really disrespected the law. He reminds them of their history as a people, of their record as God had spoken to them over and over again, first of all through Moses and then through the prophets, and he reminds them of their response. Joseph was a prophet. Who was it that got Joseph into trouble? Who rejected this man? It was the patriarchs, the founding fathers of Israel, who had tried to murder Joseph, to rub him out of the story. And Moses, whom they lauded as the greatest of all of the prophets, who was it that gave him a rough time right throughout his ministry? Look at verse 35. 'This is the same Moses, that you are saying that I've criticised, whom you rejected with the words, "Who made you ruler and judge?"'

The leaders and the prophets

The point Stephen is making is that every time God sent a ruler or a deliverer, they rejected him. 'Whether it was Joseph or Moses, whether it was the prophets, and now in these last days, God's own Son, to be a ruler and a deliverer; every time God has moved towards you, you have responded in the same way.' Look at verses 51 and 52. 'You stiff-necked people,' says Stephen. Is Stephen is getting a bit aggressive? Actually he's quoting language that you find right throughout the Old Testament. Moses uses it and the prophets use it over and over again when they're describing Israel. 'You stiff-necked people with uncircumcised hearts and ears!' 'You are acting like pagans', he's saying. 'You talk like pagans, you behave like pagans, you react like pagans. You're not reacting like those who have the temple and the law, or who respect Moses and the prophets. You people are stiff-necked. Whenever God has sent to you one who is a ruler and a deliverer, you will automatically reject him. You are like the rest of humanity.' Then he delivers his punchline: 'You are just like your fathers. You always resist the Holy Spirit! Was there ever a prophet your fathers did not persecute? They even killed those who predicted the coming of the Righteous One' (Acts 7:51-52). That was their problem. They lauded the law, but they resisted the law.

The temple and the law

A very interesting thing about the Jewish people is this: after they had been delivered from their exile in Babylon, as a result of centuries of idolatry mingled with the worship of God, they resolved that they would never lapse into idolatry again. But John Calvin says, 'The human heart is an idol factory.' And that's what happened with the Israelites. They came back to the Promised Land, they said, 'We'll never make an idol again' and they turned the temple and the law into their idols. They elevated them, the physical building and the written code. They didn't bother whether they obeyed the law or not; that's the point that Stephen is making. 'You have the law and you magnify it and boast about it and wear it on your clothes. You, the leaders of the people, you carry it around with you and you hedge it around with all kinds of rules and regulations to make sure you keep it perfectly but idolise it though you do, you do not obey God's law. Your heart is an idol factory. That's why you're aggressive towards me; because I'm touching these things that go to the very heart of your false religion.'

What is Stephen getting at? He's saying to Israel, God's church is God's people. It isn't tied to an institution or a building – he's echoing the words of Jesus to the Samaritan woman: 'A time is coming when you will worship the Father neither on this mountain (Gerizim) nor in Jerusalem. ... God is spirit, and his worshippers must worship him in spirit and in truth' (Jn. 4:23,24). God is a God without boundaries. Stephen's Christian friends listening in needed to hear that too. These believers, who'd been having their Bible studies in Jerusalem, needed to hear this because they needed to break out of the little community they'd formed and the safe environment they inhabited if the gospel was ever going to reach the world.

Stephen: a witness to Christ

Stephen's speech is not so much a defence as a testimony to Jesus. The temple, the law pointed somewhere. What he is saying to these people is that without Jesus, the law, the Old Testament, the temple, gets you nowhere. Everything that was written in the past was written with a point. Everything that had happened, happened for a purpose. All of the ritual and ceremony of Israel had been preparing them, getting the stage ready. He is saying, 'Jesus is the fulfilment of the temple.' Jesus himself had taught that: 'Destroy this temple and in three days I'll raise it again …' 'You want to meet with God, no longer do you go into a building, you come to me.' In Christ we meet with God; not in a building, not in a sanctuary, not in a temple, not in anything made by man's hands.

Christ is the righteous One

Stephen says, 'Was there ever a prophet your fathers did not persecute? They even killed those who predicted the coming of the Righteous One. And now you have betrayed and murdered him.' The word 'righteousness' means conformity to a norm. Jesus is the one who conforms to the norms of God's law; he is perfectly righteous, the perfectly innocent one.

These leaders did not want to hear that. They had just rejected Jesus. They'd been irritated when Pilate had said that he was a righteous man. If they'd heard about what the Roman centurion said at the foot of the cross, they'd have been even more irritated. They were absolutely furious when Stephen says Jesus is God's Righteous One. That means they'd accused and killed an innocent man, who unlike them had perfectly conformed to God's law. In killing him, they had been true to form and they had broken their own laws. They were the guilty parties. Christ was the Righteous One in whom all good is to be found.

I think this helps us understand people's allergy to Jesus. Why is it people can speak dispassionately about the leaders of other religions, even the most off-the-wall ones, these are all right for normal conversation but speak about the Lord Jesus Christ and people's hackles are immediately raised. Why is that? It is because everything about the Lord Jesus makes us feel uncomfortable in our sin, makes us realise that we are guilty. It makes us uncomfortable with our behaviour, our thoughts, our words, our deeds, our past, those skeletons in our cupboard. He makes us realise how far short of God's norm we have fallen. His righteousness exposes our unrighteousness. That's what is operating in this passage, whenever Stephen speaks about Jesus as the Righteous One 'that you have betrayed and murdered'. They are furious and they gnash their teeth at him. They cannot stand the idea that Jesus is the Righteous One.

Christ is the glorified One

Stephen sees Jesus standing at the right hand of God and he tells them what he sees; 'I see heaven open and the Son of Man standing at the right hand of God.' He had begun this speech by talking about the God of glory (Acts 7:2) who 'appeared to our father Abraham'; now from his own personal experience he is saying 'the God of glory has appeared to me and guess what? His name is Jesus. He is the Son of Man.' He's going for the jugular here. The God of glory, who appeared to Abraham, who now appears to Stephen, is in fact the Son of Man. The very rejected, despised, crucified, buried, now risen, now exalted Jesus, is the God of glory.

And he's there, standing at the very right hand of God. This would not be lost on these people, many of them priests in the Sanhedrin. They knew that in the old temple, once a year, one man was allowed to enter into the presence of God on earth. Here was Stephen saying 'Look, one man has now entered into the presence of God in heaven. And rather than be obliterated he is standing there at the right hand of God and he is the Son of Man.' Stephen quoting from Daniel, where the Son of Man is led into the presence of the Ancient of Days and he is given all authority and power; all of it goes to him and he is worshipped by the heavenly throng (Dan. 7:13.14). Stephen is making the most astounding claim for Jesus here.

Doesn't it say in the Bible that Jesus has sat down at the right hand of the majesty on high? Why is he standing? It may very well be that this is just for Stephen. F.F. Bruce puts it like this: 'Stephen has been confessing Christ before men, and now he sees Christ confessing his servant before God.' He's got up to receive his servant home.

Stephen is a witness to Israel. And that's not in any sense of an anti-Semitic comment. In his witness to the ancient church of the Jews, Stephen is a witness to the church of Jesus today, because Jesus is still often rejected within the organised church. We still have the tendency to hark back to the old Jewish ways. The Early Church did it, after the apostolic period: they harked back to the old Jewish ways. They wanted a temple and so they built temples, physical sanctuaries, within which God could meet with his people. They recreated an old priesthood, based on the Old Testament priesthood. They tried to recreate Judaism within Christianity because the human heart always thirsts backwards to idolatry, away from the revelation in Christ Jesus. Stephen's a witness to Israel but he's a witness to us, a warning to us: remember God is not tied to buildings but to people. And when God gives his word, he doesn't want you to make an idol out of it, he wants you to obey it.

Stephen – a witness to us

Stephen teaches us how to live for Christ. If you look back to chapter 6, he is a man who's obviously got great intelligence and yet when there is a real need within the church for someone who will make sure people are being cared for, Stephen is willing to do that job. You live for Christ if you're willing to do anything.

And Stephen's clear about the Bible's message. He has the Bible firmly in his head and he understands where the Bible's going, he's full of the Scriptures. This man knew his Bible. And he does not hold back anything that's good for the people that he's speaking to. Not only that but he's a man who senses that he lives every part of his life under Christ's eye. What came to Stephen, as he stood before his accusers that day was that he was actually standing in a greater court, before a greater judge. He was actually answerable, not to these men, but to God. What he said had to count for eternity because he was about to go into eternity.

The English reformer Hugh Latimer, the bishop of Worcester, was summoned to preach once before King Henry VIII. His views in this sermon that he preached so infuriated the king that the king demanded that he come back the next day to the chapel and preach a different sermon. Next day, Latimer returned and preached exactly the same sermon to the king. And on this occasion, King Henry, who was always a bit of an enigma, thanked Latimer for his honesty. We have a record of one of Latimer's sermons and he has written in his preamble a little note to himself; 'Latimer, you are going to speak before the high and mighty King Henry VIII who is able if he think fit to take thy life away. Be careful what thou sayest. But ... remember also, thou art about to speak before the King of Kings and Lord of Lords, take heed that thou dost not displease him.' Stephen understood that. He was speaking in the presence of a greater judge.

If you're going to live for Christ you need the spirit of Jesus. You see that in Stephen's final prayer for his enemies. 'Lord, do not hold this sin against them,' he says. Doesn't it carry all the hallmarks of those words of our Lord Jesus on the cross, 'Father, forgive them, for they do not know what they are doing'? Stephen has imbibed the spirit of his master, he is like his master; and even when the pressure is on and little time is left, what is inside the man, his spirit of Christlikeness, comes to the surface.

Dying for Christ

Stephen teaches us how to live for Christ – and Stephen teaches us how to die for Christ. The devil wants death to strip us of our confidence and throw us into confusion, to turn us to self-pity, resentment and bitterness. What God wants is that the death of the saints will be a declaration to the world of death's futility. Look at verse 55 – Stephen, full of the Holy Spirit, gazed to heaven and saw the glory of God and Jesus standing there. 'While they were stoning him, Stephen prayed, "Lord Jesus, receive my spirit." Then he fell on his knees and cried out, "Lord, do not hold this sin against them." When he had said this, he fell asleep.'

John Piper has written a great little story based on this. He says this:

It's as though, when you're dying, you're dying in a small cabin in the middle of a dark wood and as you die the door opens and you find yourself moving steadily from your death bed towards this door, this door of death. And as you move towards it you notice outside the door that there's a ravenous wolf with bare fangs and furious eyes waiting for you. At first, you're terrified. But then the Holy Spirit opens your eyes and you see just beyond the wolf, in the shadows beyond it, there is the Lord Jesus standing with one hand held out towards you, welcoming you, and in the other hand you see there is a chain and that chain is attached to a collar around the wolf's neck. And as you come towards the door, and as you're about to enter the door of death, Jesus yanks the chain, the wolf is pulled away and you go through the door into his welcoming arms.

That's the lesson that Stephen teaches us from his death; his death is full of Christ, just as his life is full of Christ. It's all of Jesus. Everything about this man, what he says, his demeanour, his humble service, his dying moments, all of it point us to the Lord Jesus Christ.

I think we settle for too little in our Christian lives these days. We don't read the biographies of people who passionately lived to be like the Lord Jesus. We play with our Christianity. When death comes, you want to be sure you are living for the right thing. At the end, Stephen 'fell asleep'. F.F. Bruce calls this an unexpectedly beautiful and sweet description of so brutal a death. You have to use big stones to kill a man. The stones that are raining down on him, they're not little pebbles ... and he falls asleep like a baby.

As the chapter concludes, we discover another thing about his death. God buries his workmen but God's work goes on. Look at verse 1: 'Saul was there, giving approval to his death.' What had Stephen taught? God is not bound. He isn't tied to the temple or the Promised Land. Here is this man who would get the message of Stephen's speech. He would take the gospel to the ends of the earth. God's word is not bound. You run your eye down the rest of chapter 8 and you find these Christians, who up to this stage have been tied to Jerusalem, suddenly get the message; persecution breaks out and they leave Jerusalem and suddenly Jesus' words to them before he went back to heaven, to take the gospel from Jerusalem to Judea, come true, as they spill out of Jerusalem into Judea. Then despised Samaria hears the gospel. By the end of chapter 8 an African hears the gospel and the message goes down to Ethiopia. Within a couple of chapters, the gospel is going to a Gentile man and the Gentile mission explodes into life. And the devil thought he'd silenced the church by silencing this one man … God buries his workman but his work goes on.

Tertullian wrote this: 'Kill us, torture us, condemn us, grind us to the dust. The more you mow us down, the more we grow. For the seed of the church is the blood of the Christian.' The rest of the book of Acts describes how that happens. We too are living in transitional times. You better be sure that what you live for is worth dying for; worth being ostracised for; worth losing your career prospects for; even worth being imprisoned for, perhaps even dying for.

Crossing Frontiers

by *Jonathan Lamb*

JONATHAN LAMB

Jonathan is presently Director of Langham Preaching for Langham Partnership International, a global programme seeking to encourage a new generation of preachers and teachers. This is a ministry which networks with national leaders in many parts of the world, including Africa, Asia and Latin America, as well as central Europe and Eurasia.

Formerly a Chairman of the Keswick Convention and Word Alive, Jonathan still serves as a Trustee of Keswick Ministries, and regularly speaks at 'Keswicks' in other countries. Apart from teaching in a variety of contexts around the world, he is also a member of the preaching team at his local church, St Andrews, in Oxford. He is the author of *Faith in the Face of Danger*, published in the Keswick series, and based on Keswick Bible Readings from Nehemiah.

Jonathan is married to Margaret and they have three daughters.

Crossing Frontiers

Acts chapter 10

Introduction

I don't know if you've made a plane journey recently but in my view the business isn't getting any easier. In quite a large number of airports these days, there are longer and more detailed security checks, there are interrogations, strip searches and forms to fill in. I made a journey last month into Eurasia and I arrived in the country and had to fill out a customs form with all kinds of questions. 'Are you carrying any fruit, plants, large amounts of foreign currency, electronic equipment, explosives, weapons or Kalashnikovs?' There was even a box which said: 'Are you carrying any radioactive materials?' In fact, it reminded me of a column which Thomas Friedman wrote a short while ago where he was going through customs like that. He imagined a couple in front of him and they were filling out the customs form and the husband said to the wife, 'Darling, did we pack the nuclear waste in your suitcase or in mine? Is the plutonium in your handbag or is it in the black duffel?'

When you think about crossing frontiers, I suppose most of us would have expected that it should be getting easier. One of the most obvious features of the world in which we live is our increasing inter-connectedness, expressed through all kinds of elements in what we

nowadays call globalisation. If the old days of the Cold War were characterised by division, the Berlin Wall, these days our world is characterised by integration; not the Wall but the Web. Some people, when
they speak about our world, imagine a far greater interconnectedness
and far fewer barriers. All the communication networks – the international travel, the worldwide web, pluralism, multi-culturalism – all
these things, they suggest, mean that there are fewer frontiers in our
increasingly interconnected world.

Yet that's not the whole story. The paradox of living in this world
is that, alongside the growing integration, there are also increasing
signs of fracture. In fact, the debate in the UK after the London
bombings included the question: why is it that distinct ethnic and religious groups fail to integrate into British society? That's a common
problem all around the world. We have seen post-communist countries in the Balkans or the former Soviet Union, or post-colonial
countries in Africa, still riven with these deep-set rivalries and ethnic
divisions. Cultural prejudice often lies behind all kinds of social and
political division in almost every continent of the world. It's expressed
in a whole variety of ways, not just in those big issues of religion and
ethnicity, here in the United Kingdom. We have our distinct nations,
whether it's Yorkshire or Cornwall or the Home Counties or
Liverpool. We find within our cities and within our neighbourhoods
that there are barriers. We might say there are cultural prejudices of all
kinds in almost every situation.

The church: with or without barriers?

One of the most exciting things about Luke's account in Acts is the
way in which the gospel of Jesus Christ, preached in the power of the
Holy Spirit, dismantled so many alienations which existed in the first
century. It hurdled over the barriers which are so evident in Scripture
and in our own culture. If you take the day of Pentecost right at the
beginning as an obvious example, remember the comments of the
crowd which gathered. 'Utterly amazed, they asked: "Are not all these
men who are speaking Galileans? Then how is it that each of us hears
them in his own native language?"' This diverse international group

that had gathered in Jerusalem heard the message in their own language, and this was a pointer of what Acts is going to show us. The Holy Spirit was breaking down barriers and was creating a new society, a new community.

What do people make of the church today? I read the criticism of the poster advertisements that have been introduced by churches, particularly to attract the 18 to 30 group. There was a full page article in *The Times* written by James Shilling, and it had this: 'Riven by ugly squabbles, ashamed of its past, uncertain of its future, the church is a thoroughly mediocre product.' Often the popular image of the church is not of some radical new society where all of these barriers have been removed. It doesn't seem to be free of prejudice but rather to be a bickering and failing institution, as far as the journalists are concerned. In contrast, Paul frequently stressed the extraordinary social inclusiveness of the new community, the church; 'There is neither Jew nor Greek, slave nor free, male nor female.'

Peter and Cornelius

We have come to a very significant moment in the story in the book of Acts. The account of the developing mission of the church focuses on this story in quite a remarkable way. It's not only quite a long chapter, but it's picked up again in chapter 11 as Peter retells it, and it's even referred to again in chapter 15. Luke sees this event as a very significant turning point in the advance of the church, particularly in the way in which it crosses frontiers. It's probably the most significant story in the whole book in terms of that issue.

There are three scenes.

Caesarea: verses 1-8

In Caesarea we're introduced to Cornelius, a centurion in the Italian Regiment. It's very clear from the opening verses that Luke wants to highlight that the Holy Spirit is already at work in this man, this Gentile Roman soldier. And in verse 2 Luke gives a remarkable description of him. 'He and all his family were devout and God-fearing; he gave generously to those in need and prayed to God regularly.' Luke is deliberate in adding phrase after phrase to show that here was a godly man. Later in the chapter in verse 27 it says that he was a leader of a larger group, which included his extended family and some soldiers, who were true seekers after God.

In this opening section, verse 4, the angel answered him, 'Your prayers and gifts to the poor have come up as a memorial offering before God.' It's a remarkable little statement about this man: we should not downplay the significance of what Luke tells us about him. John Calvin realised: 'If a small spark of faith had such a great effect on Cornelius, what ought the full splendour of knowledge be bringing about in us? But as we boast loud-mouthed of Christ, how far removed most of us are from the example of this holy man ... there is apparent scarcely a tiny shadow of the virtues which he had in abundance.'

This is a Gentile. This is not a member of God's family. I think that it's an enormously encouraging thing to mention. There is no doubt at all in the Western world that there is a great deal of moral and spiritual decline. But this passage reminds us that there are people who are still searching for the reality which only Jesus Christ can bring. And there are many opportunities still available to us as God's people to win this post-modern generation. It's confused, it's often heading in entirely the wrong direction, but there may well be such a person as Cornelius quite close to us.

The other significant thing about Cornelius which Luke is very concerned to highlight is that he is a Roman soldier; so for Palestinian Jews, this man was the enemy. Gentiles were outsiders, excluded from God's special covenant. Some of the rabbinical proverbs suggested that the Gentiles were created by God in order to serve as fuel for the flames of hell! Cornelius carried responsibilities in the army of occupation: here was a man who was a real target for hatred. But notice what happens in this first scene. God was at work in this Gentile soldier and through a vision he was told to seek out Peter, verse 5. So in verses 7 and 8 he sent his servants to Joppa.

Joppa: verses 9-23

Joppa was a predominantly Jewish town, and Peter had been there encouraging the young believers. Peter had already begun to see that there might be a wider mission for the church beyond the Jewish community. He'd mixed with all kinds of people and his Judaistic strait-jacket was beginning to be loosened (verse 6). He was staying with Simon the tanner. For orthodox Jews, leather workers were definitely considered to be amongst the unclean. So it's intriguing that Peter was staying there. And in Simon's house he had a vision that was going to transform his perspective.

It was lunchtime, he was feeling hungry and there on the roof he had a very unusual dream of a sheet descending down from heaven, containing all kinds of animals, clean and unclean, and then a voice says, 'Get up, Peter. Kill and eat.' Amongst some of those animals there were those that would disgust an orthodox Jew. Peter objects. He had never eaten anything forbidden by Jewish food laws. And the voice replies, 'Do not call anything impure that God has made clean.' Or the New Living Translation, 'If God says something is acceptable, don't say it isn't.'

Peter was obviously resistant to this message. It came several times to him. David Smith makes reference to the contrast between Cornelius and Peter at this point. 'The contrast is striking and disturbing. The man without the Bible is humbly obedient to the light given to him, while the one with all the privileges who in this case has actually walked with the incarnate word of God, resists further light and will not budge from an inherited theological position.'[7]

Luke says three times this message came to him, the voice said, 'Eat' and then the sheet disappeared back into heaven. I like Eugene Peterson's paraphrase, verse 17, 'As Peter, puzzled, sat there trying to figure out what it all meant, the men sent by Cornelius showed up.' It's a story full of supernatural co-ordination. And some people see a little humour in the text – Peter even asks the visitors if they know what's happening (verse 21). The Lord had made it very clear to Peter (verses 19, 20) that these men are coming: 'Do not hesitate to go with them, for I have sent them.' Apparently the Greek word translated 'hesitate' could also be translated 'discriminate'. 'They may be Gentiles but don't discriminate; go with them.'

---

[7] David Smith, *Mission after Christendom* (London: Darton, Longman and Todd, 2003)

Back to Caesarea: verses 23-48

Peter had come to understand that the vision that he had back in Joppa was not about clean and unclean animals. That vision was about people. Verse 28: 'You are well aware that it is against our laws for a Jew to associate with a Gentile or visit him. But God has shown me that I should not call any man impure or unclean. So when I was sent for, I came without raising any objection. May I ask why you sent for me?'

There could hardly have been a better platform for Peter's evangelistic sermon. Cornelius had gathered a large crowd of relatives and friends and after explaining the way in which God had spoken to him, that led him to call for Peter, he says, 'We're all here in the presence of God to listen to everything the Lord has commanded you to tell us' (verse 33). It's not every day that an evangelist has that kind of opportunity. So Peter begins to preach. And he begins to show that he has had 'a paradigm shift'. He's still learning on his feet, verse 34: 'I now realise how true it is that God does not show favouritism but accepts men from every nation who fear him and do what is right.'

Some people say this passage is the story of the conversion of Cornelius but equally it's the remarkable story of Peter's conversion as he began to see what God was saying to him. For a first-century Jew, this was an extraordinary change of perspective.

Three foundation truths

God accepts all

Peter said, 'I see very clearly that God doesn't show partiality. In every nation he accepts those who fear him and do what is right.'[8] There's the first foundation truth. God has no favourites. It's been said that the Jews twisted the doctrine of election into a doctrine of favouritism. They'd become filled with racial pride, even hatred. When God chose Abraham, his choice had nothing to do with elitism or exclusivism.

---

[8]   New Living Translation

God chose Abraham and his family in order to bless all the families of the earth through them. And if only the Jews had eyes to see, this global missionary purpose which God declared there to Abraham in Genesis 12 was repeated time and time again by the prophets. That was one of Isaiah's favourite themes. It was for all the nations. God's purposes, according to this passage, declare that his desire is for the rescue of all, irrespective of race, gender or economic status. Peter doesn't mean that everyone who lives a good life is on their way to heaven. He's going to make it very clear that entry into God's family is through Jesus Christ.

Jesus is Lord of all

'You know the message God sent to the people of Israel, telling the good news of peace through Jesus Christ, who is Lord of all.' The way that sentence is constructed places the emphasis on that last phrase, 'Lord of all'. It's almost as though as Peter is preaching, he finally realises Jesus is not just the Lord of the Jews, Jesus is Lord of all. His vision of Jesus until this point had been restricted. His awareness of God's mission had been distorted by his racial prejudice and his idea of God's family was too small. Jesus was not only the Messiah; he was the Saviour and the Lord of all. And he is the Judge of all, Peter explains in verse 42: 'He commanded us to preach to the people and to testify that he is the one whom God appointed as judge of the living and the dead.' All are accountable to Jesus who is the Lord and judge of all.

Salvation is available to all

Verse 43: 'All the prophets testify about him that everyone who believes in him receives forgiveness of sins through his name.' Everyone, he says; Gentiles as well as Jews. Everyone who believes in who Jesus is and what Jesus has done, everybody without exception receives forgiveness of sins. As one commentator puts it, this 'everyone' crashes through the barriers of race and nationality. It is good news for all. It is not that every religion leads us to God, that's ruled out by Peter's insistence in these verses that Jesus is Saviour and Lord and Judge of all. But the good news of salvation is for all irrespective of background.

Three visual aids

These are the three foundation truths that Peter preached and which are the basis of this new society which God has been creating ever since. There are then three visual aids that demonstrate the reality of what Peter had proclaimed.

The coming of the Spirit

Notice Peter's preaching is interrupted by the outpouring of the Spirit on everybody who was listening to him. The small group of Jewish believers were astonished to see that the Holy Spirit had been poured out 'even on the Gentiles'. That was the first visual aid – that what Peter was talking about was absolutely true. This is sometimes called the Gentile Pentecost.

Baptism

Notice verse 47, ' "Can anyone keep these people from being baptised with water? They have received the Holy Spirit just as we have." So he ordered that they be baptised in the name of Jesus Christ.' Peter insisted that these Gentile believers were baptised. He wanted to demonstrate that since they'd received the Spirit, they should not be regarded as outsiders. They were now included in the family; and baptism was the mark of family membership.

Fellowship

The third visual aid is a small reference right at the end of the chapter. I've called it fellowship because it's a further practical demonstration of the fact that the gospel crosses boundaries. Notice verse 48 tells us that Peter was invited to stay with them for a few days. In verse 23, Peter had invited the men Cornelius had sent into the house to be his guests. Jews would not wish to darken the door of Gentiles in this way but now the gospel made the difference. They were fellow members of God's family, they ate and drank together. Peter taught them more about their new-found faith and these walls of prejudice and suspicion began to fall. There is one new community, founded by the Spirit by faith in Jesus Christ.

The backlash

If you go into chapter 11, as Peter reports the news to his more conservative brethren back in Jerusalem, he's criticised. 'You went into the
home of uncircumcised men and ate with them.' Peter had to help
them to undergo the same shift of perspective, and eventually they say,
'So then, God has granted even the Gentiles repentance unto life'
(verse 18).

It was an incredible new departure in the story of the church. In
the house of Cornelius, those believers rejoiced that Jesus was the
Saviour of the world, that the Spirit was the universal Spirit, that the
unique but the universal entry point into God's family had nothing to
do with race or national privileges. It was all to do with faith in the
one Lord Jesus Christ.

Three implications

I think this is a fantastic chapter that has a great deal to say to us
believers. Let me give you the three implications.

How do we see other people?

The story of Acts is not only the story of the growth of the church,
it's especially the story of how faith in Christ breaks through religious,
racial and national boundaries. The whole book is about that. Luke is
interested to record the great diversity of people who enter the
church, all ages, both sexes, Jew and Gentile, individuals, households,
the obscure, the prominent, all the different occupations that they represented and the characters, some exalted, some people of influence,
some ordinary people. Luke deliberately demonstrated this kind of
mix. One of the clear lessons of this chapter is that we must learn to
see people as God sees people.

In 2 Corinthians 5 where Paul is talking about his ministry of reconciliation, he says in verse 16 that having met Christ, he now looks
at people differently. He says, 'So from now on we regard no-one from
a worldly point of view.' We don't judge people by the standards of this
world, by external image, nationality or culture. To recognise that Jesus

Christ died for all means that we look at people with a new perspective. Paul had even changed his view of Christ of course; before he met Jesus Christ he judged him by his own religious prejudices. Someone executed on a cross couldn't possibly be the Messiah, the deliverer for God's people. But when he met Jesus his view changed completely; he saw him now not as some obscure Galilean but as the Saviour of the world.

To be in God's family is to see people very differently. How do we see people? How do we see a Muslim? How do we see an Arab? How do we see a young black? How do we see an upper middle-class wealthy conservative? How do we see a homosexual? How do we see a transvestite? How do we see a hooker? How do we see the person who's begging on the street? If we had a vision tonight of a great sheet, what would be in the sheet that you would see? What does God want to point out to you or to me? What kind of prejudices would he want to reveal?

Paul is saying in 2 Corinthians 5, 'I will not judge people by the world's yardstick, by the prejudices of my own culture. Instead I see each person as someone whom God loves and someone whom God longs to bring into his family through the one Lord Jesus Christ.'

How do we see the church?

It's clear from this passage that in God's family there is absolutely no room for prejudice or discrimination. The church should be the one place where the divisions which mark our society are rendered completely irrelevant. I remember some years ago a friend of ours was taking her driving test. She did the hill start and as she struggled to select second gear, the examiner looked over his glasses – he obviously had a ministry of encouragement – and he said to her, 'Don't worry, love. There'll all in the same box, all you've got to do is sort them out.' And she actually managed the task and passed her test.

When she told us that phrase, 'They're all in the same box, all you've got to do is sort them out', it had a peculiarly Pauline ring as far as I was concerned. Because that's exactly what Paul says in Ephesians, 'You belong to the one Father, you are indwelt by the one Holy Spirit, you've been redeemed by the one Lord Jesus Christ, you are all in the same family, you're all in the same box.' The key issue for so much of Paul and his writing in the epistle is, 'How do you get the cogs to mesh together? How do you get this machine to work? How do you demonstrate the reality of this new society?' Acts 10 says there is no room for churches that are exclusive, exclusive to a particular class, exclusive to a particular generation, exclusive to a particular ethnic group or gender or race, there is no room for the prejudices of our upbringing or for the racial and sexual and economic discrimination of our culture.

A few years ago I visited some friends in the Balkans. It was in the midst of some of the conflict between Serbs and Croats. I remember being at a conference and Serbs, Croats and Albanians deliberately came to the platform, linked arms and sang in their languages the song 'Bind us together, Lord.' If we truly demonstrated that kind of radical community, this new society which dismantles barriers to fellowship, then we will be a very powerful witness in an increasingly fractured world. I remember John White writing on this in his book, *The Fight*.

> Christ died that humans of every type be reconciled to God and to one another. The genius of Christianity is that it makes possible ongoing fellowship between people who could not otherwise tolerate, let alone enjoy, one another. Christ gets refined socialites hobnobbing with migrant farm workers, middle-aged squares weeping with rebels and swingers, blacks and Indians and whites praying earnestly together, management and labour sharing each others' problems. In a world divided by class, commerce, race, education, politics, the generation gap and a million clashing interests, Christ alone can make incompatibles mesh.[9]

How do we view our mission?

The third implication of this passage also shouts at us: that Jesus is the Saviour of the world, that the gospel is for all. I wonder might we be slow in the task of mission because of similar prejudices to Peter? We too might wish to emphasise our doctrine of election. We've been

---

[9]   John White, The Fight (Leicester: IVP, 1977)

chosen and others apparently have not been chosen. But this doctrine of election is not the same as elitism or exclusivism. In fact, in 1 Timothy 2, Paul deliberately emphasises that God wants all people to be saved. God longs for everyone to be saved; it breaks his heart to see people walking away from him. Commenting on those verses in 1 Timothy 2, John Stott reminds us that election is usually introduced in the Bible for one of three reasons: firstly, to humble us, reminding us that the credit for our salvation belongs to God only; secondly, to reassure us, promising us that he will never let us go if we belong to him; and thirdly, to stir us to mission. God chose Abraham and his family in order to bless all families of the earth through them. So, I now quote Stott, 'election is never introduced in order to contradict the universal offer of the gospel, or to provide us with an excuse for opting out of world evangelisation.'[10] That shapes our mission, that's our agenda, that universal perspective pushes us forward in the task of sharing the good news globally.

What about the frontiers that you have immediately around you? What about the diverse communities in which we live? What about the different nations which are represented by the thousands of guests who come to this country, international students and many others, pouring into our cities? What about the stigmatised immigrant communities? What about the asylum seekers and the refugees in Europe? What about the billions who have never heard what Peter says there in verse 36, 'The good news of peace through Jesus Christ who is Lord of all.' Acts 10 is a very significant new departure in the Christian mission. We are also engaged in that task, and as we worship in our local churches we have in our minds not only the global family of God to which we belong, but also the global mission of God for which we are responsible. We're called to enjoy that fellowship and to feel that responsibility.

We'll pause just for a moment of quiet and I'll ask those three questions one more time. How do we see other people? What kind of prejudice might be lurking in our hearts? I wonder if we could name

---

[10] John Stott, *1 Timothy and Titus, The Bible speaks today* (Leicester: IVP, 1996) p64

someone in the Lord's presence, someone whom you've steered clear of before, for a whole variety of reasons; maybe in your workplace, or in your neighbourhood, but who perhaps you could connect with, remembering all that Acts 10 is teaching us. How do we see other people?

How do we see the church? Have we become something of an exclusive club where only a certain type of person is acceptable? Or are we characterised by open doors, open homes and open hearts?

And thirdly, how do we see our mission? Is our vision of Jesus too small, just like Peter's? Or are we willing to cross some of these frontiers? It might just mean crossing the street for some of us, it might mean befriending someone at work, it might even be crossing the world for others. How do we see our mission?

Into the ghetto

by Nigel Lee

NIGEL LEE

After four years teaching English, followed by twenty years on the staff of Operation Mobilisation, Nigel became leader of the student ministry of UCCF, the CU movement (1992-2000). He currently divides his time between Myton Church, Warwick, where he is an elder, and a variety of Bible teaching conferences, both in the UK and abroad. He has a consulting role with a number of churches, and is a regular broadcaster with the BBC. He and his wife Tricia have three grown-up children.

Into the ghetto

Acts chapter 14

Introduction

The picture given of UK Christianity in the media these days is one of decline. Churches are shrinking, traditional denominations are running out of money, out of clergy and out of a future. The energy is gone, the buildings are being sold off, RE lessons in school have to teach a multi-faith mishmash, and the assumptions underpinning the values of our whole society are no longer Christian, we are told.

Last week I was watching a programme on television about various New Age practices here in the Lake District. There was a shot of twelve people in a circle – dancing, chanting, meditating, holding hands and keeping a peaceful, dreamy look on their faces. That apparently was news. Three and a half thousand people in a tent like this, committed to orthodox Christianity, doesn't interest the media quite so much. The message being dripped in all the time is that Christianity is finished; no one takes it seriously any more, they're getting ready to put out the lights. The only ones left, we're told, are the wacky fringe, who walk on the ceilings in their services so that their money can drop out of their pockets into the hands of their anointed leaders. However, in my experience as I travel around the UK, something else is happening which the media and the BBC haven't fully caught on to. It's under their radar and as far as I'm concerned, long may it remain so.

New churches are springing up all over the place, often meeting in schools and secular venues, often independent, always outward-looking, always as committed to the Bible as we are here, and committed to evangelism. Some of these churches are out-plants from main denominations. Some mainline churches are looking as if Jesus was back in residence and in business again. It's wonderful to see – Anglican churches doing church planting in other parishes. Shocking! Fantastic! These new, Bible-teaching churches have increased, so I understand, by 68 per cent in the last ten years and they're fighting back in our country in a most cost-effective way. And the folk in these new churches are very good friends with evangelical people carrying on in the mainline denominations. It's a unity of Spirit, rather than of label, as expressed in the banner above our heads at this convention: 'All one in Christ Jesus'.

People who live in the vicinity of those kind of churches – warm, courageous, outward-looking fellowships – know that at the local level there is a different story to be told; one which hasn't been cottoned on to in the press. I think the future of Christianity in these islands depends upon local churches like this; local churches with certain biblical characteristics. It will not be dependent upon university theology departments; it will not be dependent upon bishops or BBC religion; it will, humanly speaking, be dependent upon local churches with something of the New Testament about them. And this means we should be thinking about church-planting back into areas where things have declined.

Which brings us to tonight's chapter because it is a chapter about church planting. Paul sets out the key essentials. How did the truths of the gospel become enfleshed in living communities that made a difference to the people around? In a book written about a hundred years ago, Roland Allen, who was an Anglican mission strategist, highlighted the difference between Paul's missionary work and ours. 'He founded churches,' said Allen, 'we found missions.' I think it's less true now than it was back then, but it's still worth reflecting on. Paul established living gospel communities all over Galatia, Macedonia, Achaia and 'Asia'. Before AD 47 there were no churches in these provinces, (what we would call western Turkey and modern-day Greece). In AD 57, Paul could speak as if his work there was done.

In the passage we read I see six steps to church planting and effective mission. At the end of the chapter, Paul is arriving back in Antioch, from where he had been sent out. Imagine the great crowd that came to listen to his story. 'We went first to Cyprus, and would you believe it, the Roman governor was converted. Then we came to Pisidian Antioch, and preached the gospel in the Jewish synagogue. Then there was a riot and we were thrown out, so we moved on to Iconium. We preached the gospel in the synagogue again, and there was another riot, and we were thrown out of Iconium. Then we all went down to Lystra. There wasn't a synagogue there so we preached the gospel in the streets and there was a third riot. I was stoned nearly to death. So we came down to Derbe, but because they thought they'd killed us in Lystra, they didn't follow us any further. So we preached there, making many disciples. Then we went back on a follow-up visit, all through those same places, and here we are, full of praise at how God has been opening a door of faith to so many people.'

I want to take you through verses 21-23 and through the six steps that Paul highlights.

1. Preach the biblical gospel

This was the strong backbone of all that Paul did. He preached God's words, not his own thoughts. This was the essential key to his impact. You find references to this bold preaching of the good news dotted throughout the chapter – verses 1, 3 (twice), 7, 9, 15, 21 and 25. Even when they knew trouble was coming, Paul and Barnabas kept on teaching God's word. Look at verses 2 and 3 – the Jews refused to believe; they stirred up the Gentiles and poisoned their minds against the brothers, so in response Paul and Barnabas spent considerable time there, just teaching Scripture.

But I want you to notice how differently Paul preached in different places, and to different audiences. In chapter 13, Paul preached to a Jewish audience in Pisidian Antioch: it's one of the longest sermons we have in Acts, and was preached in a formal religious setting. He quotes the Old Testament; he refers to the covenant, the law and to Israel's history. He brings pivotal promises from Isaiah, and he quotes from the Psalms, because his audience shared a Jewish background. When you come over to chapter 14 (verses 14-18), he's talking to Gentiles who have none of that background, so he uses none of that material. He talks about the God of creation, about the seasons, the crop cycles, the generosity of a God who cares for us. It's all equally true; it's all consistent with Scripture, but these two gospel sermons could not be more different.

We have two clear examples in the Acts of the Apostles of Paul preaching to Gentiles: here in chapter 14 he's probably talking to illiterates, and in chapter 17 he's talking to sophisticated Athenian intellectuals. Again he doesn't obviously quote Scripture. What he says, however, is entirely consistent with Scripture, and is born out of profound thinking about the word of God. He begins where people are. He talks about what was familiar, he focuses on the evidence of God's kindness, grace and power, before he ever gets to Jesus.

What counts for 'good preaching' in this country can become terribly one-dimensional. We have a lot of good preachers who would only be able to operate in the 'synagogue', delivering an uninterrupted monologue to people who already know their Bibles. We also need those who can speak to 'the Gentiles', explaining something profound in an impromptu setting at the drop of a hat.

Think about the word of God

We don't think hard enough about how to relate the gospel that is revealed and anchored in Scripture to people who haven't the vaguest notion of what it is all about. Careful thinking, combined with amazing flexibility in communication, were the driving forces behind Paul's effectiveness in church-planting; and not only church-planting, but church sustaining. It's comparatively easy to start a church in this country. You get half a dozen disaffected people from other local churches, and you begin in your living room. It has been done hundreds of times. The problem is sustaining it. What always seems to be lacking is someone prepared to do the hard work of thinking deeply and carefully about Scripture, combined with developing great flexibility in communication. It is always the word of God that does the work of God in the end.

In this regard I have a great burden that we should not become over-reliant for our training of Bible teachers upon the Bible colleges. I'm not saying anything against the Bible colleges – it's simply that most people won't go near them, they haven't the time, and can't afford it. We all need to be thinking more carefully about Scripture, getting it into our bloodstream and working out how to use it. The effective advance of the gospel requires the word of God to take root, not just in a few elite professionals, a new monochrome priesthood, but in all of us.

We all need to be committed to the study, storing and sharing of Scripture. That's a challenge! Many of us, especially when we reach middle-age, become bored with the word of God. We let the preaching of it depend upon others and we switch off from the hard work that's required. It is only as the word of God is fuelling us, changing us, driving our minds, that things will go back into growth mode in this country. It won't happen by just listening to a few professional, paid preachers. I'm sure *their* greatest longing is that more people would begin to engage with the word of God in a way that would bubble out of them, challenging and 'outthinking' our secular culture.

2. Make disciples

Paul made many (verse 21). We have a problem: it's called 'canteen Christianity'. People take a little of this, a little of that, they half belong to a church, they might try another one next week, or they just go along to listen, not to be changed. Paul did not set out to make mere listeners, pew-fillers or spectators. This is a particular challenge, I suspect, to churches with very good preachers, because they tend unwittingly to train their congregations to be very good listeners, and not much else. There isn't enough life change. Preachers love roomfuls of docile listeners. The more that come, the happier they are. But it's difficult for them to know what remains in a listener's mind the following week; what is affecting his home life or his business and so on.

I remember being asked years ago to lead an evangelistic mission in Cambridge University. At that time the students there were listening to some of the finest preachers in the country. But when it came to finding those who were going to roll up their sleeves and get their hands dirty in the mission, it was a different story. Many students had begun to treat Christianity as if it was largely about listening to lectures. We must not allow this strong, and essential, emphasis on teaching the word of God to merely produce passive listeners. Paul made disciples, who impacted the Roman empire in time. His business wasn't merely like a bit of Feng Shui in the brain, shuffling the furniture about, but not making much difference. Acts 2:42 strikes the key note of New Testament discipleship. The first Christians were 'devoted' to being part of a learning church, a loving and serving church, a cross-centred church and a praying church. It became a burning passion for Paul to see the gospel produce disciples who would make disciples like that.

It is sometimes taught that Paul's strategy was to head for the big cities, preach the gospel, start a church, and then that church would automatically start other satellite churches around. It is an over-simplification. The basic strategy of Paul was to trust in the guidance of the Holy Spirit, and to go looking to make disciples wherever. Chased out of Iconium, which was quite a big city, he went to Lystra, some tiny place up in the mountains. When Paul was chased out of huge Thessalonica, he went to tiny Berea, and started making disciples.

Here in rural Lystra, Paul connects with someone who would go on to be a cracker of a disciple, Timothy. Years later, in Philippians 2:20, he says of Timothy, 'I've got no-one else like him. Everyone else seems to attend to their own interests in the end but not this man Timothy. He attends to the interests of Jesus Christ.' Paul's work of making disciples like Timothy, not merely listeners, was a key to his church planting. It is, in fact, what the Lord Jesus told us to be doing. 'Don't you worry about building the church; I'll build the church. You go and make disciples who will obey me.'

3. Give purposeful encouragement

Paul 'strengthened and encouraged these disciples to remain true to the faith' (verse 22). There's an extraordinary verse in Luke 22:43. In the garden of Gethsemane Jesus is agonising in prayer and 'an angel from heaven appeared to him and strengthened him'. How would you set about strengthening Jesus, the Son of God? What do you think that angel did, in order to fulfil that responsibility? Did he remind him of home, of heaven, its atmosphere, its certainties? Did the angel remind him of his Father, his purposes, his promises? Did the angel remind him of the word of God that he had come to obey?

Would there be any parallels in the way Paul set about strengthening and encouraging these disciples? What would you have done? Teach them Scriptures with strong application? Give warnings, if needed? Answer questions? Spend time with them? Remind them of the promises of God? Show them the example of how all this is to be lived? Tell of what brothers and sisters in other places are experiencing?

Notice he wanted to see them strong in loyalty to 'the faith', to its content, its foundation stones. Sometimes we can avoid being morally disloyal to the gospel but gradually become intellectually disloyal. He wanted them loyal to 'the faith' as he had preached it. He strengthened them in their grasp of the truth.

4. Prepare for hardship

Paul prepared these disciples to go through persecution (verse 22b). He taught them to expect to go through it, not to dodge around it, because a commitment to Jesus and his word will always lead to opposition, in one way or another. Just look through the chapter: verse 2, the Jews deliberately poisoned the minds of the Gentiles against the Christians. Verse 4, they split the city against them. Verse 5, they hatched plots to ill-treat them. In verses 11 to 13 there was a serious misunderstanding to deal with. 'They're gods!' said the local people for a while. Then minutes later, 'Oh … not gods? Then let's kill them!' Paul had to cope with these massive swings in public opinion.

When the Jews arrived down from Iconium, he was battered unconscious (verse 19). The next day when he came round, he set out to walk sixty miles to Derbe. Can you imagine Paul back on his follow-up visit weeks later, standing in front of these young Christians with the scars still raw on him? Maybe his eyesight had been damaged, after the stones had come flying in. 'This is the way it is. I love these people. If this is what it's going to take to reach them for Christ, OK.' What a powerful reminder that would have been that we go through these hardships for the sake of the kingdom of God.

I lived for a while in Kathmandu, back when it was illegal for a Nepali to become a Christian. He could do a year in prison for becoming a Christian, and six years for leading anyone else to Christ. There were times when some of our Nepali friends wanted to be baptised and we would go with them up into the mountains, posting lookouts. Then we would dam a stream to create enough water to get them under. The lookouts would warn us if anyone was coming. After the baptisms had taken place, the stone dam would be broken and the water would flow as if nothing had happened. The men getting baptised knew what they were facing, they were courageous and ready for hardship. Only a couple of years ago I was speaking in a pastors' conference in Nepal, to men now leading the growing churches there. I had never been in a room with so many battered old jail-birds! Most of them had done time for the sake of the gospel. When those men stood in front of their congregations to talk about what it costs to be a servant of the king, and what faithfulness really means, people knew they knew what they were talking about. And when they lifted their voices in praise to God it was no cheap sound coming from their hearts.

I was in Australia last year. Around some of the big cities, particularly on the east and southeast coasts, there are dangerous bush fires from time to time. The remarkable thing about the Australian gum tree is that when it gets thoroughly charred and blackened by fire, and you think it's finished, it just sheds its blackened old bark and starts again. In a year or two it's sprouting green and getting back to normal. I suspect that significant advances in the kingdom of God cannot be made without scars of one sort or another. Probably more of them inside us than outside. These things will either happen before any great advance, or they will be the kick back afterwards. Perhaps there are hundreds of us here tonight who have been hurt or scorched by fires started deliberately by our brothers and sisters. I simply want to say to you, in Jesus' name, shed your burnt bark. Let it drop off. Don't live the rest of your life with blackened bark, just because you've been through a church split, or you've been sacked from some organisation, or you've been through some pain that probably shouldn't have happened, but it did. We need to be people, like the Australian gum tree, who shed their blackened bark and get on with reproducing and growing, forgiving and making disciples.

5. Appoint the right leaders

They 'appointed elders in each church with prayer and fasting' (verse 23). Without true spiritual leadership, churches will stagnate and lose direction. Paul saw this as absolutely vital. Otherwise people drift around in a church just doing the same things, and the main aim of the minister rises no higher than just getting everyone to come back next week. These New Testament churches had leaders that were chosen by Paul with prayer and fasting to ensure the continuation of his missionary vision.

There was a time in our own church's experience a few years ago when we had three working shepherds in the church from local farms. One Sunday I asked them in front of everyone, 'What are the essentials of a shepherd's job? What are your key responsibilities?' It took them less than one minute to highlight five things. Firstly, of course, he has to ensure a good food supply. Secondly, he must give protection from predators, whether they be foxes, stray dogs or various diseases that can get in. Thirdly, a good shepherd will keep his flock clean, as sheep, unlike some animals, are not good at cleaning themselves. Fourthly, he will attend very carefully to reproduction. A well cared-for flock on good land will tend towards producing twins, or even occasionally triplets. And finally our shepherds agreed they had a responsibility to make sure the sheep knew them, were comfortable with them, and recognised their voices. Sheep aren't very long-sighted, but they can learn to recognise voices nearby.

We need godly leaders in our churches who are committed and skilled in providing the food that people need, and in keeping folks protected from theological stuff that will bring disease. Leaders need to keep people clean from the divisions and quarrels that make us dirty and worn down. Leaders attend to multiplication: if the flock isn't breeding there is something wrong. And finally we need leaders who are out and about so that their voice is heard among the sheep; shepherds, not just managers or lecturers.

Half the passages on qualifications for church leadership in the New Testament (1 Tim 3, Titus 2, 1 Peter 5) are given to statements of who is *disqualified*. God is saying, 'These are the kinds of people I don't want anywhere near the leadership of my flock.' When Titus was left in Crete (Titus 1:5-9) to appoint elders, after Paul had preached the gospel then left, he was given a checklist of four things to look for. 'Look for those who have an exemplary home life, as far as possible (verse 6), who respond well under pressure and stress (verses 7,8), who have a good testimony in their work place (verse 7), and who have a firm grasp of the gospel, and can teach it (verse 9).' If you've got some of those in the church they are the ones to appoint as elders. If you haven't, you need to pray for them.

6. Leave!

Paul and Barnabas committed these young churches, with their elders, to the Lord in whom they had put their trust, and left (verse 23). They didn't try to control everything from then on. They said, 'These people belong to the Lord, we've given them shepherds to lead them, the Lord himself will keep watch. The leaders have to take responsibility; they will learn on the job. You see, the core truths of the gospel, if properly preached and understood, will anchor the faith of these young disciples and will go on to shape their whole future growth. This gospel has the power within itself to run and run if allowed to do so.' As Paul said, 'It is the power of God unto salvation.'

What a wonderful report back that must have been. 'We saw churches started, we saw undoubted opposition, we made disciples, we told them the truth unflinchingly. It's wonderful that God has opened a door of faith to the Gentiles.' That's a fascinating description of 'faith', isn't it? It's like a door that has been opened for you. Don't just stand there looking at it. Have you yourself gone through? Have you peered in, but then not wanted to move? There could be people here for whom God has opened that door of faith, but you're still on the outside. True believers are those that have stepped in through the door. You come inside to his family. In this message lies God's power to change you personally, and the power to create communities of heaven on earth, and in the meantime to alter the whole trajectory of society. There isn't any other message that can do this in the world. May this message feed us, anchor us and send us out to be change-makers and church planters.

Life change
by David Cook

DAVID COOK

David has been Principal of Sydney Missionary and Bible college for twenty years. He has recently retired from the chairmanship of the Katoomba Christian Convention, after thirteen years. KCC is the equivalent of the Keswick Convention in Sydney. David is the author of several books, including *Starting strong, staying strong* and *The Unheeded Christ*. His interests include cricket, rugby (union and league), good coffee and his family. He has been married to Maxine for thirty-four years and they have five adult children and four grandchildren.

Life change

Acts 26

Introduction

A mother felt it necessary to send a note along to the school to excuse her son's absence. 'Willy can't come,' the note said, 'because he hasn't been. I've given him something to make him go but until he's been, he can't come. Please excuse him.' The headmaster had to fill in the gaps. Things which go without saying need to be said.

Luke leaves very little unsaid. He emphasises the things which are important to him. Very often when you come to the book of Acts, you come to prove a point. Presbyterians come to the book of Acts to prove that churches should be ruled by elders; Anglicans come to the book of Acts to prove that churches should be ruled by bishops; Congregationalists come to the book of Acts to show that congregations should rule the church; Baptists come to the book of Acts to prove adult baptism by immersion; Presbyterians and Anglicans come to the book of Acts to prove that it's possible to baptise children of believing parents; charismatics come to the book of Acts to justify their experience; non-charismatics come to the book of Acts to justify their non-experience. Everybody is coming to the book of Acts to prove one point or another. However, for Luke none of these things are central to his purpose. So what is central to his purpose?

Keep your finger there in Acts 26 and let's go back to Luke 24 and look at that key linking verse from volume 1 to volume 2: verse 47. Remember that the Lord Jesus said, 'This is what is written: (Lk. 24:46) The Christ will suffer and rise from the dead on the third day,' and lest you think that the early church got it right from the day of Pentecost on – let me read verse 47 to you in the way the early church and the apostles understood verse 47. 'And repentance and forgiveness of sins will be preached in his name to the Jews of all nations beginning in Jerusalem.' Peter and the other apostles had to have a special vision to understand that the gospel wasn't just for Jews, but was the gospel of the universal Lordship of Christ and was for the people of all nations: Jews and non-Jews.

In the book of Acts there are twenty-one direct words from God and sixteen of those direct words from God are words directed to the apostles ordering the church to move out, to keep broadcasting the gospel. 'Do not become a huddle, jump over that ethnic barrier, the gospel is for everyone.' We should not idealise the first century and think that the century we live in is particularly difficult. We talk as if post-modernism were something unique to today. The first century was a post-modern time. Everybody had their own religion, everybody was expected by the Romans to tolerate everybody else; you could do your own thing as a Christian as long as you allowed everybody else to do their thing. Yet the apostles bring the gospel into that post-modern age and they declare Jesus. They make it clear that Christianity is not a sect of Judaism, they're not bringing along a new law. It is not spiritism, or a political movement. It was not some philosophical movement. They were proclaiming Jesus and, in Jesus, the resurrection of the dead.

The shortest definition of the gospel in the New Testament is found in Galatians, where Paul says 'We went away around preaching him'; him, Christ, the son of David, the Lord, the Author of life, the Leader, the Saviour, the holy and righteous one. This gospel must never change. This is the unchanging gospel. This is at the heart of what Luke is saying and God's directive is 'Keep taking it out.'

When one of the first missionaries, who was with Hudson Taylor in China, was about to report back to Scotland on his first furlough,

Hudson Taylor said, 'You are so full of China that when you get back to Scotland, you'll tell them about China. Don't tell them about China, tell them about Jesus and he'll look after China.' Our focus is Jesus. We are to proclaim him as Saviour, as Lord, the holy and righteous one.

In New Guinea, the gospel came to many of the tribes in the central highlands of New Guinea just after World War Two. The gospel came to a group around the Tari area of New Guinea, the Huli people. In the Huli culture, when a man is married to a woman, they are enemies. They do not live together; they have sexual relations out in the jungle and from her point of view those relations are to be endured. They live in two separate settlements, the children are raised by the mother for the first five years, and then the boys go and live with the father, but the girls stay with their mother. The two have nothing to do with one another. When the missionaries went into the Tari area to minister to the Huli people, they did not preach morality, they did not preach biblical family relationships, they preached Jesus. Jesus looked after morality. What a breakthrough it was when the first Huli man moved into the same hut and lived with his wife and set up a Christian household. It was a remarkable testimony, the work of God's grace, but the focus of the missionary was to preach Jesus, not to preach morality.

Luke is showing us here that this gospel transcends all boundaries and changes people deeply. Throughout the book of Acts, Luke underlines the things that are important, and the things that are important he repeats. As you go through the book of Acts, the Holy Spirit comes on the Jews at Pentecost in chapter 2 and then he comes on the Samaritans in chapter 8, and then he comes on the Gentile world in Cornelius' house in chapter 10 because this is a major movement. Luke gives us three reports of the coming of the Holy Spirit; not one Pentecost but three Pentecosts.

The gospel comes to the Gentile Cornelius in chapter 10, but Luke repeats a full account of what happened in chapter 11 and then he gives us another account in chapter 15. In chapter 15, where the Christians must decide whether or not they are to add a religious rite like circumcision to the gospel to make it the full gospel, and they'd come to the conclusion by sending a letter to the churches that the gospel is not to be added to or subtracted from, then Luke tells us what the letter said in chapter 15 and then he tells us again what the letter said later in chapter 15 and then he repeats it in chapter 21 and tells us what the letter said because this is an important thing. Luke underlines the important events of his narrative because he tells us not once or twice but three times.

The conversion of Saul: recording 1

That's the way it is with the conversion of Saul. It's been read to us tonight from chapter 26 but you can go back to chapter 22 and there it is again and the first record of it is in chapter 9. This is a conversion which is going to change our history and the history of the world.

This is the apostle who is our apostle. He is the first apostle to bring the gospel to Europe and from Europe the gospel went to the United States and to Australia. The gospel came to us because our apostle went there. Europe's greatness came upon it when it embraced the truth which our apostle brought to it as he declared the truth in response to the vision of the man of Macedonia. By God's grace, Paul met the risen Christ on the Damascus Road, and God sent him out in those missionary journeys to Europe and the gospel went on and the history of the world was changed.

Let's look at this significant conversion, in Acts chapter 9. Saul is a persecuting Pharisee. We first meet him in Acts chapter 8 where he's giving approval to Stephen's death. He's a Pharisee who understands clearly that works-based salvation cannot co-exist with faith-based salvation and the coming of the new means the end of the old and that's what drives his persecuting zeal. He gets letters of authority from the high priest, to deal with the heretics as far off as two hundred miles away from Jerusalem at Damascus. Notice what he says here, verses 3-6. 'As he neared Damascus on his journey, suddenly a light from heaven flashed around him. He fell to the ground and he heard a voice say to him,' in the Aramaic, literally, '"Saul, Saul, why do you persecute me?"' Notice that the voice solemnly repeats his name. Saul, a good Pharisee, who knew his Scriptures, knew that something was happening here that was quite unusual, that God was speaking to him. In order to get his attention, God repeats the name – 'Saul, Saul.'

'Why do you persecute me?' It's irrational. What is it that you find so offensive about me? In Sydney we have a radio commentator. Recently something went wrong in the studio and he let out the name Jesus Christ as a blasphemy. What is it about Jesus that this man finds so offensive? I mean if he'd have said 'Oh Adolf Hitler!' I'd understand it! But he didn't. It's totally irrational.

Notice what Jesus says to Saul here, verse 4. It's personal. 'Why is it that you are persecuting me?' It's continuous. Notice Saul's response in verse 5. He asks another question – 'Who are you?' Jesus could have said, 'I'm God.' Saul would come back, 'I want you to know that I'm persecuting those lousy Christians!' But Jesus identifies himself by his earthly name and later on we read that he actually said, 'I'm Jesus of Nazareth,' his earthly address. In one response our apostle knows that the crucified one lives and there is solidarity between him and his people.

Now I want to tell you that what Saul learned, Paul never forgot. And of the two great lessons that Saul learned and that Paul never forgot is, firstly, the greatness of grace. Saul was a persecutor and it may well be that many had died, like Stephen, as a direct result of Saul's persecuting zeal. Paul never forgot God's amazing grace. The Lord Jesus could have come and swept him away but he didn't. He comes and calls him by name: 'Saul, Saul, why?' The blinding light, the voice from heaven: Saul was having a theophany, a vision of God, the Lord Jesus was coming. And it was by grace. He did nothing to deserve it. No wonder Paul said 'By grace we are saved through faith.' What Saul learned, Paul never forgot.

Notice the second thing that Saul learned and that Paul never forgot: the solidarity between Christ and his church. Jesus said to him 'Why are you persecuting me?' 'But I'm persecuting those Christians.' 'To persecute them is to persecute me.'

On May Day in Australia we have the Trade Unionists march through the street – 'the workers united will never be defeated' solidarity. What remarkable solidarity we have here – the Lord Jesus says,

'You persecute them, with your letters and credentials from the high priest, and I take it personally.' The great lesson that the apostle Paul was learning here was that he was now located in Christ. He was no longer Adam's man; he was now Christ's man. His identity was completely changed. To be Christ's man meant, and to be Christ's people meant, that the way you treat his people is a direct reflection of the way you treat Christ.

Saul's blinded and God says to Ananias, 'Go to him.' Ananias obviously knows that he's come to persecute people so he's reluctant to go, but when Ananias goes, Paul receives his sight and he is baptised and, verse 20, 'At once he began to preach in the synagogues that Jesus is the Son of God.' That must have been an incredible Saturday morning when you turned up for the synagogue expecting the persecuting Saul and hearing the preaching Paul. What does God say to him, verse 15? 'You are my chosen instrument. You are going to take the gospel to the Gentiles.'

Saul's conversion: recording 2

Flip over now to chapter 22: the second recording of this conversion. This time Paul is before his fellow Jews in Jerusalem, who have already sought to stone him to death. He is telling them his conversion experience, verse 20:

> And when the blood of your martyr Stephen was shed, I stood there giving my approval and guarding the clothes of those who were killing him. Then the Lord said to me, 'Go; I will send you far away to the Gentiles.' The crowd listened to Paul until he said this. Then they raised their voices and shouted, 'Rid the earth of him! He's not fit to live!'

What was the sticking point in Jerusalem? It was this: they could accept what Paul was saying up to a point, but once he says that Yahweh's purposes are not just with Jews and Israel but actually with the Gentiles, they grit their teeth and say 'Rid the world of him!' How could God have a purpose for the Gentiles?

Saul's conversion: recording 3

Now go over to chapter 26. We're with Governor Festus and King Agrippa is there with his wife Bernice. King Agrippa controlled the area of Galilee but the Roman governor Festus controlled Jerusalem, Judea and Samaria. And Paul repeats his experience. But now he gives a fuller treatment to his commissioning, verse 16.

> Now get up … on your feet. I have appeared to you to appoint you as a servant and as a witness of what you have seen of me and what I will show you. I will rescue you from your own people and from the Gentiles. I am sending you to them to open their eyes and turn them from darkness to light, and from the power of Satan to God, so that they may receive forgiveness of sins and a place among those who are sanctified by faith in me.

Paul tells this august company that he has been faithful to that heavenly vision, verse 20. He goes on in his message, verse 23, 'I preached that the Christ would suffer and as the first to rise from the dead would proclaim light to his own people and to the Gentiles.' Whereas the sticking point in chapter 22 was the point where he says 'Yahweh commissioned me to go to the Gentiles' notice that the sticking point here before the Gentile court comes when he talks about the resurrection of the dead. At this point Festus interrupted Paul's defence and says, 'You're out of your mind, Paul! Your great learning is driving you insane.' This idea that God should raise the dead fascinated them in Acts chapter 17 in Athens: death was the great unknown and the Athenian philosophers, the Stoics and the Epicureans wanted to know more about this resurrection of the dead.

Notice in chapter 26:8, Paul signals to Agrippa that this is the real issue: 'O King, it is because of this hope that the Jews are accusing me. Why should any of you consider it incredible that God raises the dead?' Notice, here is the resurrection. The apostle Paul doesn't avoid it. He seeks to explain it. It doesn't go without saying. It is the key issue but it sticks in the experience of Festus who simply says, 'You're out of your mind.'

Recently I was talking to a man in Sydney and he asked me if he was going to become a Christian, did he have to believe that Jonah was in the belly of a fish for three days? I said, 'In order to become a Christian, you need to believe that God raised Jesus from the dead. Believe that in your heart and confess it with your mouth and you'll be saved. Let's focus on that. Jonah will come later.'

Here is the resurrection of the dead. The Gentiles, lots of the Jews, they didn't like the idea. That's the issue that stuck with them. I remember I was doing some post-graduate work at university in Sydney, a course on cosmology. One night we were looking at the Pythagoreans and at one point in the lecture, this lecturer said, 'Do you know, I'd be a Pythagorean if I weren't a Christian.' And there was a lady in the group and she said, 'Why are you a Christian?' 'I'm a Christian because I'm a historian. I cannot explain the resurrection of Jesus in any way but that he was actually raised from the dead: that's why I'm a Christian.' It's the core issue.

Remember that young solicitor, that young lawyer, Frank Morrison? He decided that he was going to disprove Christianity once and for all and if he could just disprove the resurrection of Jesus he knew that he would win his case. He sat down as a lawyer and he sifted through all the evidence. And he became a committed Christian, convicted that the legal evidence was all there, it was true, and he wrote *Who moved the stone?*[11]

Paul says here 'Why should any of you think it's incredible that God raises the dead?' Of course he raises the dead! If you do not believe that God raised the Lord Jesus from the dead, how do you account for the Holy Spirit being poured out on those three people groups? And those Jews from all those nations being able to speak in all those languages without ever going to a language laboratory? How do you account for that? How do you account for that man who had not walked being raised to walk in chapter 3 of Acts if Jesus had not been raised from the dead? And what about Paul? Don't tell me it was just wishful thinking on his part! He didn't want to meet Jesus, he was out to persecute his followers! Who do you think

[11] Frank Morison, *Who moved the Stone?* (London: Faber and Faber, 1975)

appeared to him on the Damascus Road, when he says it was Jesus? All this is building up our case for the resurrection of Jesus. I don't leave my brain at the door when I become a Christian. It's because I've got a brain and God has opened me to see the truth of this, that Jesus was raised from the dead.

And so this question we've come to says, 'Why should any of you consider it incredible that God raises people from the dead?' But Festus interrupts, 'You're mad! Your learning is driving you insane!' 'No,' Paul says, 'I am not insane,' verse 25. 'What I am saying is true and reasonable. The king's familiar with these things, he'll tell you about it. God prophesied he'd do this and he's done it. Look, I'm here; I'm the sign that he's done it. I'm one of the signs. I'm telling you I've heard and seen the risen Christ.'

Don't slink away from the resurrection. A lot of people say, 'You're insane about the resurrection. If I see Jesus die, and then rise, I'll believe.' That's scientific evidence. But we all recognise that there's another kind of evidence. If I go before a magistrate, and I've had an accident in my car, the magistrate doesn't say, 'Let's run these cars apart from each other and I'll watch and you run them into each other again.' He says, 'Let me hear what the witnesses have got to say.' That's legal evidence. We've got all the legal evidence we need. Paul says, 'I saw him. The other apostles saw him. Over five hundred believers, most of whom are still alive, saw him. How much more evidence do you need? Who poured the Spirit out from the right hand of God, if it was not the resurrected and ascended Jesus? Who made this man walk, if it was not the resurrected Jesus? Who did appear, claiming to be Jesus on the Damascus Road, if it wasn't the resurrected Jesus? Listen to the legal evidence.'

Agrippa put two and two together, 'Do you think that in such a short time you can persuade me to be a Christian?' This bloke knows that Paul's got a persuasive argument! Paul says, 'This is my goal. Short time or long, I pray that not only you but everybody listening to me will become what I am' that is, a Christian. That's Paul's goal. Luke wants us to come away from chapter 26 to see that the Roman legal system has given Paul a good hearing and the Roman legal system has given its verdict, verse 32: 'This man could have been set free'

– he's quite innocent of any charge – 'except that he has appealed to Caesar.'

The response to the gospel

Do not be surprised when people are both unreasoning and unreasonable in their response to the gospel. Keep praying and keep persevering. Remember what happened with Stephen. They couldn't stand up to his wisdom in debate and so they secretly trumped up some false charges against him. Do not ever be surprised at what happens; the unreasoning and unreasonableness of our opponents. I know a scientist who tells me that the Bible is untrue; it's a lot of rubbish. I say, 'Have you read it?' 'No because it's untrue and it's a lot of rubbish.' A good scientist, eh?

'You're out of your mind!' That's what so many say. Look back at Acts chapter 17. Paul has come to the Areopagus, verse 31, there's the summary of what he says. God 'has set a day when he will judge the world with justice by the man he has appointed. He has given proof of this to all men by raising [that man] from the dead.'

Paul is saying God has set the day. He's given proof that the day has been set, so repent – that is wisdom. Notice what Luke tells us here in verse 32: some sneered. There will be those who sneer. There will be those who say, 'We want to hear more about this,' and there will be those for whom it was a never-to-be-forgotten day: Dionysus and Damaris, and a number of others who came to know Christ.

Expect a difficult time

Life is not easy for the apostle Paul. There is no vestige of prosperity theology here. One-third of the book of Acts is about Paul's trials, from chapter 21 through to 28; his court cases, his stonings, his rejections by his own people. They want to tear him apart. Then the snake bites him, then he is shipwrecked. The message is that ministry will be tough, so get ready for it. But God buries his messengers but never his message. Keep it up.

What God has joined together … let not man separate. It's an incredible thing, isn't it, that in the wedding service, there comes that moment; 'As a minister of the church of Jesus Christ, and having heard you exchange your vows of love and faithfulness, I now declare you to be husband and wife in the name of the Father, the Son, and the Holy Spirit. What God has joined together, let no man separate.' It's an awesome moment, in the midst of a wonderful moment of joy and happiness: what God has joined together, husband and wife, let no man separate. What God has joined together, Jesus, Saviour and Lord, don't separate. What God has joined together, justification and its fruit in sanctification, don't separate. What God has joined together in the life of the apostle Paul, conversion and commissioning, don't separate.

Do you see yourself as the slave of this gospel? Is that your vocation? Are you living in order to send and support? Or are you living as one who is sent and supported? The necessary application of this passage is, 'Am I a servant of this gospel like Paul? Do I have the beautiful feet to take this gospel to the ends of the earth?'

In Sydney we are blessed by having an Anglican diocese which is evangelical. Our archbishop there said, 'I want to make it a goal unto God that we should pray and work for that 10 per cent of the population of Sydney, that is, 450,000 people, should be in Bible-believing churches in Sydney.' It's a great goal and they changed their budget accordingly and you know when churches change their budgets accordingly, they're serious about it! But that's what they're working for and the Anglicans are planting churches all over our great city.

What is the danger of that? The danger of that is that we become so focused on Sydney that we forgot the needs of the world. In Sydney our college is full; it has never been fuller in its history. The Anglican theological college in Sydney is full, it has never been fuller in its history. And yet we are training so many people for ministry that it's a challenge to the church to employ them. We need to build bigger and bigger teams in our churches. It's a sign of success to have a big ministry team. It might just be a sign of greed. What about the needs of the world?

Very often I'm invited to go to churches and speak at missionary conferences and I often have to say to the church, 'The best thing that this church can do to forward the cause of world mission is to sack its missionary committee.' Why do we have missionary committees as though missions is an appendage of what we're really on about? Either sack the mission committee or make the central governing body of the church the missions committee. Because at every point the church needs to be thinking mission – how can we get this gospel to the ends of the earth? How can we get it out there? The direct speech of God in the book of Acts, 'out, out, out'.

Did you know that 90 per cent of paid Christian workers in the world today minister to 30 per cent of the world's population? That means that 10 per cent of paid Christian workers minister to 70 per cent of the world's population. Do you see the injustice in that? Are you praying regularly, writing regularly to those who are out there? Are you giving in a way that is self-sacrificial? If you'd got Paul here, and you cut Paul, he would bleed gospel. And if you cut the church we are to bleed gospel.

In the front of my Bible I've got this and I like to see it every day.

> When I reach the end of my days, a moment or two from now, I must look backward on something more meaningful than the pursuit of houses, land, stocks, bonds. I will consider my earthly existence to have been wasted unless I can recall a loving family, a consistent investment in the lives of people, and an earnest attempt to serve the God who made me. Nothing else makes much sense.

Where are your beautiful feet going to take you?

Keswick 2005

Tapes, videos, CDs and books

All talks recorded at Keswick 2005 plus many more audio and video recordings from the Keswick Convention dating back to 1957 can be ordered from www.iccspreadingtheword.com
Catalogues and price lists of audio tapes of the Keswick Convention platform and seminar ministry, including much that is not included in this book, can be obtained from

ICC
Silverdale Road
EASTBOURNE
Sussex
BN20 7AB
Tel: 01323 643341
Fax: 01323 649240

www.iccspreadingtheword.com

Details of videos and CDs of selected sessions can also be obtained from the above address.
Some previous annual Keswick volumes (all published by STL/Authentic media) can be obtained from:
The Keswick Convention Centre, Skiddaw Street,
KESWICK, Cumbria, CA12 4BY

Tel: 017687 80075
www.keswickministries.org

or from your local Christian bookseller or direct from the publishers, Authentic Media, 9 Holdom Avenue, Bletchley, Milton Keynes, MK1 1QR. Tel: 01908 364200 – or from www.wesleyowen.com

Keswick 2006

Week 1 15th – 21st July
Week 2 22nd – 28th July
Week 3 29th July – 5th August

The annual Keswick Convention takes place in the heart of the English Lake District, an area of outstanding natural beauty. It offers an unparalleled opportunity for listening to gifted Bible exposition, meeting Christians from all over the world and enjoying the grandeur of God's creation. Each of the three weeks has a series of morning Bible readings, and then a varied programme of seminars, lectures, literary lunches, prayer meetings, concerts, drama and other events throughout the day, with evening meetings that combine worship and teaching. There is also a full programme for children and young people, and a special track for those with learning difficulties which takes place in week 2. K2, the interactive track for those in their twenties and thirties, also takes place in week 2.

The theme for Keswick 2006 is **The Church in the Power of the Spirit** and speakers confirmed so far are:

Chris Wright of Langham Preaching International who will give the Bible readings in week 1; **Ajith Fernando** of YFC who will give the Bible readings in week 2, and **Nigel Lee** who will give the Bible readings in week 3. Other confirmed speakers are **Steve Brady, Dave Fenton, Liam Goligher, Jonathan Lamb, Peter Lewis, Peter Maiden, Amy Orr-Ewing, Luis Palau, Derek Tidball** and **Keith White**.

For further information, please contact:

The Operations manager
Keswick convention centre
Skiddaw Street
Keswick
Cumbria
CA12 4BY

Tel: 017687 80075

Email: info@keswickministries.org

Website: www.keswickministries.org